M000303403

Baby's First Year

A THOUGHT-A-DAY JOURNAL

RENE J. SMITH

ILLUSTRATED BY
DAVID COLE WHEELER

PETER PAUPER PRESS, INC.
WHITE PLAINS, NEW YORK

Designed by David Cole Wheeler

Copyright © 2011
Peter Pauper Press, Inc.
202 Mamaroneck Avenue
White Plains, NY 10601
All rights reserved
ISBN 978-1-4413-0567-1
Printed in China
7 6 5 4 3 2

Visit us at www.peterpauper.com

Welcome, Baby!

Baby: You're here at last and off on your first-year adventure. Learn to sleep through the night! Discover solid foods! Train the folks to make funny faces! And let them record it all in this no-pressure, on-the-go, day-by-day journal. *Baby's First Year: A Thought-a-Day Journal* takes the stress out of recording your most precious moments. (Hey, your new parents need all the help they can get!)

Parents: This easy-to-use journal makes a unique keepsake record of Baby's very first year. Convenient page-a-day format allows you to record quick notes about bringing up Baby! Use it to take notes about feedings, changings, sleep patterns, baby's mood, and special moments. And include your own thoughts and impressions about each day—joys, challenges, mood, and more.

Keep the journal on your nightstand or take it along in the stroller or car. Use it as your exclusive baby journal or as a place to record things you want to detail later in your "official" baby book. *Baby's First Year: A Thought-a-Day Journal* also includes Monthly Calendar/Progress Pages in the back to record Baby's height, weight, and monthly highlights, plus a back pocket and an elastic band place holder.

Daily Pages

Babies are such a nice way to start people.

DON HEROLD

Date

....

Notes for Today

_____
_____
_____
_____
_____
_____
_____
_____
_____
_____

Feeding

_____
_____
_____

Changing

_____
_____
_____

Sleep/Naps

_____
_____
_____

Parent's Day: ☐ Extra crazy! ☐ Survival Mode ☐ OK

☐ Good ☐ Super easy!

Baby's Mood	Your Mood
☹ ☹ ☺ ☺ ☺	☹ ☹ ☺ ☺ ☺

Date

....

Notes for Today

_____
_____
_____
_____
_____
_____
_____
_____
_____
_____

Feeding

_____
_____

Changing

_____
_____

Sleep/Naps

_____
_____

Parent's Day: ☐ Extra crazy! ☐ Survival Mode ☐ OK
☐ Good ☐ Super easy!

Baby's Mood	Your Mood
☹ 😕 😐 🙂 😊	☹ 😕 😐 🙂 😊

Date

....

Notes for Today

_____
_____
_____
_____
_____
_____
_____
_____
_____

Feeding

_____
_____

Changing

_____
_____

Sleep/Naps

_____
_____

Parent's Day: ☐ Extra crazy! ☐ Survival Mode ☐ OK
☐ Good ☐ Super easy!

Baby's Mood	Your Mood
☹ 😖 😐 🙂 😊	☹ 😖 😐 🙂 😊

Date

....

Notes for Today

_____
_____
_____
_____
_____
_____
_____
_____
_____
_____

Feeding
_____
_____

Changing
_____
_____

Sleep/Naps
_____
_____

Parent's Day: ☐ Extra crazy! ☐ Survival Mode ☐ OK

☐ Good ☐ Super easy!

Baby's Mood	Your Mood
☹ 😐 😐 🙂 ☺	☹ 😐 😐 🙂 ☺

Date

....

Notes for Today

_____
_____
_____
_____
_____
_____
_____
_____
_____
_____
_____

Feeding

_____
_____

Changing

_____
_____

Sleep/Naps

_____
_____

Parent's Day: ☐ Extra crazy! ☐ Survival Mode ☐ OK

☐ Good ☐ Super easy!

Baby's Mood	Your Mood
☹ 😕 😐 🙂 😊	☹ 😕 😐 🙂 😊

Date

....

Notes for Today

_____
_____
_____
_____
_____
_____
_____
_____
_____

Feeding

_____
_____

Changing

_____
_____

Sleep/Naps

_____
_____

Parent's Day: ☐ Extra crazy! ☐ Survival Mode ☐ OK
☐ Good ☐ Super easy!

Baby's Mood	Your Mood
☹ 😕 😐 🙂 😊	☹ 😕 😐 🙂 😊

Date

....

Notes for Today

_____
_____
_____
_____
_____
_____
_____
_____
_____
_____

Feeding

_____
_____

Changing

_____
_____

Sleep/Naps

_____
_____

Parent's Day: ☐ Extra crazy! ☐ Survival Mode ☐ OK
              ☐ Good   ☐ Super easy!

Baby's Mood	Your Mood
☹ 😐 😐 🙂 😊	☹ 😐 😐 🙂 😊

Date

....

Notes for Today

_____
_____
_____
_____
_____
_____
_____
_____
_____
_____

Feeding

_____
_____
_____

Changing

_____
_____
_____

Sleep/Naps

_____
_____
_____

Parent's Day: ☐ Extra crazy! ☐ Survival Mode ☐ OK
              ☐ Good   ☐ Super easy!

Baby's Mood   Your Mood
😣 😒 😐 🙂 😊   😣 😒 😐 🙂 😊

Date

....

Notes for Today

_____
_____
_____
_____
_____
_____
_____
_____
_____
_____

Feeding

_____
_____

Changing

_____
_____

Sleep/Naps

_____
_____

Parent's Day: ☐ Extra crazy! ☐ Survival Mode ☐ OK

☐ Good ☐ Super easy!

Baby's Mood	Your Mood
😣 😖 😐 🙂 😊	😣 😖 😐 🙂 😊

Date

....

Notes for Today

_____
_____
_____
_____
_____
_____
_____
_____
_____

Feeding

_____
_____

Changing

_____
_____

Sleep/Naps

_____
_____

Parent's Day: ☐ Extra crazy! ☐ Survival Mode ☐ OK

☐ Good ☐ Super easy!

Baby's Mood	Your Mood
😖 😣 😐 🙂 😊	😖 😣 😐 🙂 😊

Date

....

Notes for Today

_____
_____
_____
_____
_____
_____
_____
_____
_____

Feeding

_____
_____

Changing

_____
_____

Sleep/Naps

_____
_____

Parent's Day: ☐ Extra crazy! ☐ Survival Mode ☐ OK
☐ Good ☐ Super easy!

Baby's Mood	Your Mood
☹ 😐 😐 🙂 😊	☹ 😐 😐 🙂 😊

Date

....

Notes for Today

_____
_____
_____
_____
_____
_____
_____
_____
_____

Feeding

_____
_____

Changing

_____
_____

Sleep/Naps

_____
_____

Parent's Day: ☐ Extra crazy! ☐ Survival Mode ☐ OK

☐ Good ☐ Super easy!

Baby's Mood	Your Mood
😣 😔 😐 🙂 😊	😣 😔 😐 🙂 😊

Date

....

Notes for Today

_____
_____
_____
_____
_____
_____
_____
_____
_____
_____

Feeding

_____
_____

Changing

_____
_____
_____

Sleep/Naps

_____
_____
_____

Parent's Day: ☐ Extra crazy!   ☐ Survival Mode   ☐ OK

☐ Good   ☐ Super easy!

Baby's Mood	Your Mood
☹ 😐 😐 🙂 😊	☹ 😐 😐 🙂 😊

Date

....

Notes for Today

_____
_____
_____
_____
_____
_____
_____
_____
_____
_____

Feeding

_____
_____
_____

Changing

_____
_____
_____

Sleep/Naps

_____
_____
_____

Parent's Day: ☐ Extra crazy! ☐ Survival Mode ☐ OK

☐ Good ☐ Super easy!

Baby's Mood	Your Mood

Date

....

Notes for Today

_____
_____
_____
_____
_____
_____
_____
_____
_____
_____
_____

Feeding

_____
_____

Changing

_____
_____

Sleep/Naps

_____
_____

Parent's Day: ☐ Extra crazy! ☐ Survival Mode ☐ OK
               ☐ Good   ☐ Super easy!

Baby's Mood	Your Mood
☹ 😐 😐 🙂 😊	☹ 😐 😐 🙂 😊

Date

....

Notes for Today

_____
_____
_____
_____
_____
_____
_____
_____
_____
_____

Feeding

_____
_____
_____

Changing

_____
_____
_____

Sleep/Naps

_____
_____
_____

Parent's Day: ☐ Extra crazy! ☐ Survival Mode ☐ OK

☐ Good ☐ Super easy!

Baby's Mood	Your Mood
😣 😫 😐 🙂 😊	😣 😫 😐 🙂 😊

Date

....

Notes for Today

_____
_____
_____
_____
_____
_____
_____
_____
_____
_____

Feeding

_____
_____
_____

Changing

_____
_____
_____

Sleep/Naps

_____
_____
_____

Parent's Day: ☐ Extra crazy! ☐ Survival Mode ☐ OK
☐ Good ☐ Super easy!

Baby's Mood	Your Mood
☹ 😑 😐 🙂 😊	☹ 😑 😐 🙂 😊

Date

....

Notes for Today

_____
_____
_____
_____
_____
_____
_____
_____
_____
_____

Feeding

_____
_____

Changing

_____
_____

Sleep/Naps

_____
_____

Parent's Day: ☐ Extra crazy! ☐ Survival Mode ☐ OK

☐ Good ☐ Super easy!

Baby's Mood	Your Mood
☹ 😕 😐 🙂 ☺	☹ 😕 😐 🙂 ☺

Date

....

Notes for Today

_____
_____
_____
_____
_____
_____
_____
_____
_____

Feeding

_____
_____

Changing

_____
_____

Sleep/Naps

_____
_____

Parent's Day: ☐ Extra crazy! ☐ Survival Mode ☐ OK

☐ Good ☐ Super easy!

Baby's Mood	Your Mood
😣 😖 😐 🙂 😊	😣 😖 😐 🙂 😊

Date

....

Notes for Today

_____
_____
_____
_____
_____
_____
_____
_____
_____
_____

Feeding

_____
_____

Changing

_____
_____

Sleep/Naps

_____
_____

Parent's Day: ☐ Extra crazy! ☐ Survival Mode ☐ OK
☐ Good ☐ Super easy!

Baby's Mood	Your Mood
☹ ☹ ☺ ☺ ☺	☹ ☹ ☺ ☺ ☺

Date

....

Notes for Today

_____
_____
_____
_____
_____
_____
_____
_____
_____
_____

Feeding

_____
_____
_____

Changing

_____
_____
_____

Sleep/Naps

_____
_____
_____

Parent's Day: ☐ Extra crazy! ☐ Survival Mode ☐ OK

☐ Good ☐ Super easy!

Baby's Mood	Your Mood
☹ 😕 😐 🙂 😊	☹ 😕 😐 🙂 😊

Date

....

Notes for Today

_____
_____
_____
_____
_____
_____
_____
_____
_____

Feeding

_____
_____

Changing

_____
_____

Sleep/Naps

_____
_____

Parent's Day: ☐ Extra crazy! ☐ Survival Mode ☐ OK

☐ Good ☐ Super easy!

Baby's Mood	Your Mood
😣 😖 😐 🙂 😊	😣 😖 😐 🙂 😊

Date

··

Notes for Today

_____
_____
_____
_____
_____
_____
_____
_____
_____
_____

Feeding

_____
_____
_____

Changing

_____
_____
_____

Sleep/Naps

_____
_____
_____

Parent's Day: ☐ Extra crazy! ☐ Survival Mode ☐ OK

☐ Good ☐ Super easy!

Baby's Mood	Your Mood
☹ 😕 😐 🙂 😊	☹ 😕 😐 🙂 😊

Date

....

Notes for Today

_____
_____
_____
_____
_____
_____
_____
_____
_____
_____

Feeding

_____
_____
_____

Changing

_____
_____
_____

Sleep/Naps

_____
_____
_____

Parent's Day: ☐ Extra crazy! ☐ Survival Mode ☐ OK

☐ Good ☐ Super easy!

Baby's Mood	Your Mood
☹ 😖 😐 🙂 😊	☹ 😖 😐 🙂 😊

Date

....

Notes for Today

_____
_____
_____
_____
_____
_____
_____
_____
_____

Feeding

_____
_____

Changing

_____
_____

Sleep/Naps

_____
_____

Parent's Day: ☐ Extra crazy! ☐ Survival Mode ☐ OK
☐ Good ☐ Super easy!

Baby's Mood	Your Mood
☹ 😐 😐 🙂 😊	☹ 😐 😐 🙂 😊

Date

....

Notes for Today

_____
_____
_____
_____
_____
_____
_____
_____
_____

Feeding

_____
_____

Changing

_____
_____

Sleep/Naps

_____
_____

Parent's Day: ☐ Extra crazy! ☐ Survival Mode ☐ OK
☐ Good ☐ Super easy!

Baby's Mood	Your Mood
😣 😖 😐 🙂 😊	😣 😖 😐 🙂 😊

Date

....

Notes for Today

_____
_____
_____
_____
_____
_____
_____
_____
_____
_____

Feeding

_____
_____

Changing

_____
_____

Sleep/Naps

_____
_____

Parent's Day: ☐ Extra crazy!   ☐ Survival Mode   ☐ OK
☐ Good   ☐ Super easy!

Baby's Mood	Your Mood
☹ 🙁 😐 🙂 😊	☹ 🙁 😐 🙂 😊

Date

....

Notes for Today

_____
_____
_____
_____
_____
_____
_____
_____
_____

Feeding

_____
_____
_____

Changing

_____
_____
_____

Sleep/Naps

_____
_____
_____

Parent's Day: ☐ Extra crazy! ☐ Survival Mode ☐ OK
☐ Good ☐ Super easy!

Baby's Mood   Your Mood
☹ 😕 😐 🙂 ☺   ☹ 😕 😐 🙂 ☺

Date

....

Notes for Today

_____
_____
_____
_____
_____
_____
_____
_____
_____
_____

Feeding
_____
_____
_____

Changing
_____
_____
_____

Sleep/Naps
_____
_____
_____

Parent's Day: ☐ Extra crazy! ☐ Survival Mode ☐ OK
☐ Good ☐ Super easy!

Baby's Mood	Your Mood
😣 😖 😐 🙂 😊	😣 😖 😐 🙂 😊

Date

....

Notes for Today

_____
_____
_____
_____
_____
_____
_____
_____
_____

Feeding

_____
_____

Changing

_____
_____

Sleep/Naps

_____
_____

Parent's Day: ☐ Extra crazy! ☐ Survival Mode ☐ OK

☐ Good ☐ Super easy!

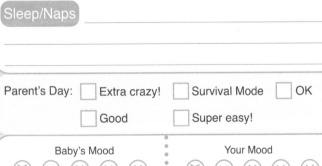

Baby's Mood ☹ ☺ ... Your Mood ☹ ☺

Date

....

Notes for Today

_____
_____
_____
_____
_____
_____
_____
_____
_____

Feeding

_____
_____

Changing

_____
_____

Sleep/Naps

_____
_____

Parent's Day: ☐ Extra crazy!   ☐ Survival Mode   ☐ OK

☐ Good   ☐ Super easy!

Baby's Mood	Your Mood
☹ 😕 😐 🙂 😊	☹ 😕 😐 🙂 😊

Date

....

Notes for Today

_____
_____
_____
_____
_____
_____
_____
_____
_____

Feeding

_____
_____

Changing

_____
_____

Sleep/Naps

_____
_____

Parent's Day: ☐ Extra crazy! ☐ Survival Mode ☐ OK

☐ Good ☐ Super easy!

Baby's Mood	Your Mood
☹ 😕 😐 🙂 😊	☹ 😕 😐 🙂 😊

Date

....

Notes for Today

_____
_____
_____
_____
_____
_____
_____
_____

Feeding

_____
_____

Changing

_____
_____

Sleep/Naps

_____
_____

Parent's Day: ☐ Extra crazy! ☐ Survival Mode ☐ OK

☐ Good ☐ Super easy!

Baby's Mood	Your Mood
😫 😕 😐 🙂 😊	😫 😕 😐 🙂 😊

Date

....

Notes for Today

_____
_____
_____
_____
_____
_____
_____
_____
_____

Feeding

_____
_____

Changing

_____
_____

Sleep/Naps

_____
_____

Parent's Day: ☐ Extra crazy! ☐ Survival Mode ☐ OK

☐ Good ☐ Super easy!

Baby's Mood	Your Mood
☹ 😦 😐 🙂 ☺	☹ 😦 😐 🙂 ☺

Date

....

Notes for Today

_____
_____
_____
_____
_____
_____
_____
_____
_____

Feeding

_____
_____
_____

Changing

_____
_____
_____

Sleep/Naps

_____
_____
_____

Parent's Day: ☐ Extra crazy! ☐ Survival Mode ☐ OK

☐ Good ☐ Super easy!

Baby's Mood	Your Mood
☹ 😐 😐 🙂 ☺	☹ 😐 😐 🙂 ☺

Date

....

Notes for Today

_____
_____
_____
_____
_____
_____
_____
_____
_____
_____

Feeding

_____
_____

Changing

_____
_____

Sleep/Naps

_____
_____

Parent's Day: ☐ Extra crazy! ☐ Survival Mode ☐ OK
☐ Good ☐ Super easy!

Baby's Mood	Your Mood
☹ 😐 😐 🙂 😊	☹ 😐 😐 🙂 😊

Date

....

Notes for Today

_____
_____
_____
_____
_____
_____
_____
_____
_____

Feeding

_____
_____
_____

Changing

_____
_____
_____

Sleep/Naps

_____
_____
_____

Parent's Day: ☐ Extra crazy! ☐ Survival Mode ☐ OK
              ☐ Good   ☐ Super easy!

Baby's Mood	Your Mood
☹ ☺	☹ ☺

Date

....

Notes for Today

_____
_____
_____
_____
_____
_____
_____
_____
_____
_____

Feeding

_____
_____

Changing

_____
_____

Sleep/Naps

_____
_____

Parent's Day: ☐ Extra crazy! ☐ Survival Mode ☐ OK

☐ Good ☐ Super easy!

Baby's Mood	Your Mood
😖 😔 😐 🙂 😊	😖 😔 😐 🙂 😊

Date

....

Notes for Today

_____
_____
_____
_____
_____
_____
_____
_____
_____

Feeding

_____
_____
_____

Changing

_____
_____
_____

Sleep/Naps

_____
_____
_____

Parent's Day: ☐ Extra crazy! ☐ Survival Mode ☐ OK
              ☐ Good   ☐ Super easy!

Baby's Mood	Your Mood
☹ ☹ ☺ ☺ ☺	☹ ☹ ☺ ☺ ☺

Date

....

Notes for Today

_____
_____
_____
_____
_____
_____
_____
_____
_____

Feeding

_____
_____
_____

Changing

_____
_____
_____

Sleep/Naps

_____
_____
_____

Parent's Day: ☐ Extra crazy! ☐ Survival Mode ☐ OK

☐ Good ☐ Super easy!

Baby's Mood	Your Mood
☹ 😕 😐 🙂 ☺	☹ 😕 😐 🙂 ☺

Date

....

Notes for Today

_____
_____
_____
_____
_____
_____
_____
_____
_____
_____

Feeding

_____
_____
_____

Changing

_____
_____
_____

Sleep/Naps

_____
_____
_____

Parent's Day: ☐ Extra crazy! ☐ Survival Mode ☐ OK
☐ Good ☐ Super easy!

Baby's Mood	Your Mood
☹ 🙁 😐 🙂 😊	☹ 🙁 😐 🙂 😊

Date

....

Notes for Today

_____
_____
_____
_____
_____
_____
_____
_____
_____

Feeding

_____
_____

Changing

_____
_____

Sleep/Naps

_____
_____

Parent's Day: ☐ Extra crazy! ☐ Survival Mode ☐ OK

☐ Good ☐ Super easy!

Baby's Mood	Your Mood
☹ 😐 😐 🙂 😊	☹ 😐 😐 🙂 😊

Date

....

Notes for Today

_____
_____
_____
_____
_____
_____
_____
_____
_____
_____

Feeding

_____
_____

Changing

_____
_____

Sleep/Naps

_____
_____

Parent's Day: ☐ Extra crazy! ☐ Survival Mode ☐ OK
              ☐ Good   ☐ Super easy!

Baby's Mood	Your Mood
😣 😖 😐 🙂 😊	😣 😖 😐 🙂 😊

Date

....

Notes for Today

_____
_____
_____
_____
_____
_____
_____
_____
_____

Feeding

_____
_____
_____

Changing

_____
_____
_____

Sleep/Naps

_____
_____
_____

Parent's Day: ☐ Extra crazy! ☐ Survival Mode ☐ OK

☐ Good ☐ Super easy!

Baby's Mood	Your Mood
☹ 😕 😐 🙂 😊	☹ 😕 😐 🙂 😊

Date

....

Notes for Today

_____
_____
_____
_____
_____
_____
_____
_____
_____
_____

Feeding

_____
_____
_____

Changing

_____
_____
_____

Sleep/Naps

_____
_____

Parent's Day: ☐ Extra crazy! ☐ Survival Mode ☐ OK

☐ Good ☐ Super easy!

Baby's Mood	Your Mood
☹ 😕 😐 🙂 😊	☹ 😕 😐 🙂 😊

Date

....

Notes for Today

_____
_____
_____
_____
_____
_____
_____
_____
_____
_____

Feeding

_____
_____
_____

Changing

_____
_____
_____

Sleep/Naps

_____
_____
_____

Parent's Day: ☐ Extra crazy! ☐ Survival Mode ☐ OK

☐ Good ☐ Super easy!

Baby's Mood
☹ 😐 😐 🙂 😊

Your Mood
☹ 😐 😐 🙂 😊

Date

....

Notes for Today

_____
_____
_____
_____
_____
_____
_____
_____
_____
_____

Feeding

_____
_____

Changing

_____
_____

Sleep/Naps

_____
_____

Parent's Day: ☐ Extra crazy! ☐ Survival Mode ☐ OK

☐ Good ☐ Super easy!

Baby's Mood	Your Mood
☹ 😐 😐 🙂 😊	☹ 😐 😐 🙂 😊

Date

....

Notes for Today

_____
_____
_____
_____
_____
_____
_____
_____

Feeding

_____
_____
_____

Changing

_____
_____
_____

Sleep/Naps

_____
_____

Parent's Day: ☐ Extra crazy! ☐ Survival Mode ☐ OK

☐ Good ☐ Super easy!

Baby's Mood	Your Mood
😣 😖 😐 🙂 😊	😣 😖 😐 🙂 😊

Date

....

Notes for Today

_____
_____
_____
_____
_____
_____
_____
_____
_____
_____

Feeding

_____
_____

Changing

_____
_____

Sleep/Naps

_____
_____

Parent's Day: ☐ Extra crazy! ☐ Survival Mode ☐ OK

☐ Good ☐ Super easy!

Baby's Mood   Your Mood

☹ ☺ ☺ ☺ ☺   ☹ ☺ ☺ ☺ ☺

Date

....

Notes for Today

_____
_____
_____
_____
_____
_____
_____
_____
_____
_____

Feeding

_____
_____

Changing

_____
_____

Sleep/Naps

_____
_____

Parent's Day: ☐ Extra crazy! ☐ Survival Mode ☐ OK

☐ Good ☐ Super easy!

Baby's Mood	Your Mood
😣 😐 😐 🙂 😊	😣 😐 😐 🙂 😊

Date

....

Notes for Today

_____
_____
_____
_____
_____
_____
_____
_____
_____

Feeding

_____
_____

Changing

_____
_____

Sleep/Naps

_____
_____

Parent's Day: ☐ Extra crazy!   ☐ Survival Mode   ☐ OK

☐ Good   ☐ Super easy!

Baby's Mood	Your Mood
☹ 😐 😐 🙂 😊	☹ 😐 😐 🙂 😊

Date

....

Notes for Today

_____
_____
_____
_____
_____
_____
_____
_____

Feeding

_____
_____
_____

Changing

_____
_____
_____

Sleep/Naps

_____
_____
_____

Parent's Day: ☐ Extra crazy!   ☐ Survival Mode   ☐ OK
☐ Good   ☐ Super easy!

Baby's Mood	Your Mood
😣 😖 😐 🙂 😊	😣 😖 😐 🙂 😊

Date

....

Notes for Today

_____
_____
_____
_____
_____
_____
_____
_____
_____

Feeding

_____
_____

Changing

_____
_____

Sleep/Naps

_____
_____

Parent's Day: ☐ Extra crazy!   ☐ Survival Mode   ☐ OK
              ☐ Good   ☐ Super easy!

Baby's Mood	Your Mood
☹ 😖 😐 🙂 😊	☹ 😖 😐 🙂 😊

Date

....

Notes for Today

_____
_____
_____
_____
_____
_____
_____
_____
_____
_____

Feeding

_____
_____

Changing

_____
_____

Sleep/Naps

_____
_____

Parent's Day: ☐ Extra crazy! ☐ Survival Mode ☐ OK
☐ Good ☐ Super easy!

Baby's Mood	Your Mood
☹ ☹ ☺ ☺ ☺	☹ ☹ ☺ ☺ ☺

Date

....

Notes for Today

_____
_____
_____
_____
_____
_____
_____
_____
_____

Feeding
_____
_____

Changing
_____
_____

Sleep/Naps
_____
_____

Parent's Day: ☐ Extra crazy! ☐ Survival Mode ☐ OK

☐ Good ☐ Super easy!

Baby's Mood	Your Mood
☹ ☹ ☺ ☺ ☺	☹ ☹ ☺ ☺ ☺

Date

....

Notes for Today

_____
_____
_____
_____
_____
_____
_____
_____
_____

Feeding

_____
_____

Changing

_____
_____

Sleep/Naps

_____
_____

Parent's Day: ☐ Extra crazy! ☐ Survival Mode ☐ OK

☐ Good ☐ Super easy!

Baby's Mood	Your Mood
😣 😔 😐 🙂 😊	😣 😔 😐 🙂 😊

Date

··

Notes for Today

_____
_____
_____
_____
_____
_____
_____
_____
_____
_____

Feeding

_____
_____
_____

Changing

_____
_____
_____

Sleep/Naps

_____
_____
_____

Parent's Day: ☐ Extra crazy!   ☐ Survival Mode   ☐ OK

☐ Good   ☐ Super easy!

Baby's Mood	Your Mood
☹ 😐 😐 🙂 😊	☹ 😐 😐 🙂 😊

Date

....

Notes for Today

_____
_____
_____
_____
_____
_____
_____
_____
_____
_____

Feeding

_____
_____

Changing

_____
_____

Sleep/Naps

_____
_____

Parent's Day: ☐ Extra crazy!   ☐ Survival Mode   ☐ OK
☐ Good   ☐ Super easy!

Baby's Mood	Your Mood
😣 😖 😐 🙂 😊	😣 😖 😐 🙂 😊

Date

....

Notes for Today

_____
_____
_____
_____
_____
_____
_____
_____
_____

Feeding

_____
_____

Changing

_____
_____

Sleep/Naps

_____
_____

Parent's Day: ☐ Extra crazy! ☐ Survival Mode ☐ OK

☐ Good ☐ Super easy!

Baby's Mood	Your Mood
😣 😕 😐 🙂 😊	😣 😕 😐 🙂 😊

Date

....

Notes for Today

_____
_____
_____
_____
_____
_____
_____
_____

Feeding

_____
_____

Changing

_____
_____

Sleep/Naps

_____
_____

Parent's Day: ☐ Extra crazy! ☐ Survival Mode ☐ OK

☐ Good ☐ Super easy!

Baby's Mood
☹ 😕 😐 🙂 😊

Your Mood
☹ 😕 😐 🙂 😊

Date

....

Notes for Today

_____
_____
_____
_____
_____
_____
_____
_____
_____

Feeding

_____
_____
_____

Changing

_____
_____
_____

Sleep/Naps

_____
_____
_____

Parent's Day: ☐ Extra crazy! ☐ Survival Mode ☐ OK
☐ Good ☐ Super easy!

Baby's Mood
☹ ☹ 😐 🙂 ☺

Your Mood
☹ ☹ 😐 🙂 ☺

Date

....

Notes for Today

_____
_____
_____
_____
_____
_____
_____
_____
_____

Feeding

_____
_____

Changing

_____
_____

Sleep/Naps

_____
_____

Parent's Day: ☐ Extra crazy! ☐ Survival Mode ☐ OK

☐ Good ☐ Super easy!

Baby's Mood   Your Mood
☹ 😕 😐 🙂 😊   ☹ 😕 😐 🙂 😊

Date

....

Notes for Today

_____
_____
_____
_____
_____
_____
_____
_____
_____
_____

Feeding

_____
_____

Changing

_____
_____

Sleep/Naps

_____
_____

Parent's Day: ☐ Extra crazy! ☐ Survival Mode ☐ OK
☐ Good ☐ Super easy!

Baby's Mood	Your Mood
☹ 😕 😐 🙂 😊	☹ 😕 😐 🙂 😊

Date

....

Notes for Today

_____
_____
_____
_____
_____
_____
_____
_____

Feeding

_____
_____

Changing

_____
_____

Sleep/Naps

_____
_____

Parent's Day: ☐ Extra crazy! ☐ Survival Mode ☐ OK

☐ Good ☐ Super easy!

Baby's Mood	Your Mood
☹ 😕 😐 🙂 😊	☹ 😕 😐 🙂 😊

Date

....

Notes for Today

_____
_____
_____
_____
_____
_____
_____
_____
_____

Feeding

_____
_____
_____

Changing

_____
_____
_____

Sleep/Naps

_____
_____
_____

Parent's Day: ☐ Extra crazy! ☐ Survival Mode ☐ OK

☐ Good ☐ Super easy!

Baby's Mood	Your Mood
☹ ☺ ☺ ☺ ☺	☹ ☺ ☺ ☺ ☺

Date

....

Notes for Today

_____
_____
_____
_____
_____
_____
_____
_____
_____

Feeding

_____
_____

Changing

_____
_____

Sleep/Naps

_____
_____

Parent's Day: ☐ Extra crazy!   ☐ Survival Mode   ☐ OK

☐ Good   ☐ Super easy!

Baby's Mood   Your Mood
😖 😕 😐 🙂 😊   😖 😕 😐 🙂 😊

Date

....

Notes for Today

_____
_____
_____
_____
_____
_____
_____
_____
_____

Feeding

_____
_____

Changing

_____
_____

Sleep/Naps

_____
_____

Parent's Day: ☐ Extra crazy! ☐ Survival Mode ☐ OK

☐ Good ☐ Super easy!

Baby's Mood	Your Mood
☹ 😐 😐 🙂 😊	☹ 😐 😐 🙂 😊

Date

....

Notes for Today

_____
_____
_____
_____
_____
_____
_____
_____
_____

Feeding

_____
_____

Changing

_____
_____

Sleep/Naps

_____
_____

Parent's Day: ☐ Extra crazy! ☐ Survival Mode ☐ OK

☐ Good ☐ Super easy!

Baby's Mood	Your Mood
😣 😖 😐 🙂 😊	😣 😖 😐 🙂 😊

Date

....

Notes for Today

_____
_____
_____
_____
_____
_____
_____
_____
_____

Feeding

_____
_____

Changing

_____
_____

Sleep/Naps

_____
_____

Parent's Day: ☐ Extra crazy!   ☐ Survival Mode   ☐ OK
              ☐ Good   ☐ Super easy!

Baby's Mood	Your Mood
☹ 😐 😐 🙂 😊	☹ 😐 😐 🙂 😊

Date

....

Notes for Today

_____
_____
_____
_____
_____
_____
_____
_____
_____

Feeding

_____
_____
_____

Changing

_____
_____
_____

Sleep/Naps

_____
_____
_____

Parent's Day: ☐ Extra crazy! ☐ Survival Mode ☐ OK
☐ Good ☐ Super easy!

Baby's Mood	Your Mood
😣 😦 😐 🙂 😊	😣 😦 😐 🙂 😊

Date

....

Notes for Today

_____
_____
_____
_____
_____
_____
_____
_____
_____

Feeding

_____
_____

Changing

_____
_____

Sleep/Naps

_____
_____

Parent's Day: ☐ Extra crazy! ☐ Survival Mode ☐ OK
☐ Good ☐ Super easy!

Baby's Mood	Your Mood
☹ 😕 😐 🙂 ☺	☹ 😕 😐 🙂 ☺

Date

....

Notes for Today

_____
_____
_____
_____
_____
_____
_____
_____
_____

Feeding

_____
_____
_____

Changing

_____
_____
_____

Sleep/Naps

_____
_____
_____

Parent's Day: ☐ Extra crazy! ☐ Survival Mode ☐ OK

☐ Good ☐ Super easy!

Baby's Mood	Your Mood
😣 😖 😐 🙂 😊	😣 😖 😐 🙂 😊

Date

....

Notes for Today

_____
_____
_____
_____
_____
_____
_____
_____
_____
_____

Feeding

_____
_____
_____

Changing

_____
_____
_____

Sleep/Naps

_____
_____
_____

Parent's Day: ☐ Extra crazy! ☐ Survival Mode ☐ OK
               ☐ Good   ☐ Super easy!

Baby's Mood	Your Mood
☹ 😐 😐 🙂 😊	☹ 😐 😐 🙂 😊

Date

....

Notes for Today

_____
_____
_____
_____
_____
_____
_____
_____
_____
_____

Feeding

_____
_____

Changing

_____
_____

Sleep/Naps

_____
_____

Parent's Day: ☐ Extra crazy! ☐ Survival Mode ☐ OK
☐ Good ☐ Super easy!

Baby's Mood	Your Mood
😖 😕 😐 🙂 😊	😖 😕 😐 🙂 😊

Date

....

Notes for Today

_____
_____
_____
_____
_____
_____
_____
_____
_____
_____

Feeding

_____
_____

Changing

_____
_____

Sleep/Naps

_____
_____

Parent's Day: ☐ Extra crazy! ☐ Survival Mode ☐ OK
☐ Good ☐ Super easy!

Baby's Mood	Your Mood
☹ 😐 😐 🙂 ☺	☹ 😐 😐 🙂 ☺

Date

....

Notes for Today

_____
_____
_____
_____
_____
_____
_____
_____
_____

Feeding

_____
_____
_____

Changing

_____
_____
_____

Sleep/Naps

_____
_____
_____

Parent's Day: ☐ Extra crazy! ☐ Survival Mode ☐ OK
☐ Good ☐ Super easy!

Baby's Mood	Your Mood
😖 😕 😐 🙂 😊	😖 😕 😐 🙂 😊

Date

....

Notes for Today

_____
_____
_____
_____
_____
_____
_____
_____
_____
_____
_____

Feeding

_____
_____
_____

Changing

_____
_____
_____

Sleep/Naps

_____
_____
_____

Parent's Day: ☐ Extra crazy!   ☐ Survival Mode   ☐ OK

☐ Good   ☐ Super easy!

Baby's Mood ☹ 😐 😐 🙂 😊   Your Mood ☹ 😐 😐 🙂 😊

Date

Notes for Today

_____
_____
_____
_____
_____
_____
_____
_____
_____

Feeding

_____
_____

Changing

_____
_____

Sleep/Naps

_____
_____

Parent's Day: ☐ Extra crazy! ☐ Survival Mode ☐ OK
☐ Good ☐ Super easy!

Baby's Mood   Your Mood
☹ ☹ ☺ ☺ ☺   ☹ ☹ ☺ ☺ ☺

Date

....

Notes for Today

_____
_____
_____
_____
_____
_____
_____
_____
_____

Feeding

_____
_____

Changing

_____
_____

Sleep/Naps

_____
_____

Parent's Day: ☐ Extra crazy! ☐ Survival Mode ☐ OK

☐ Good ☐ Super easy!

Baby's Mood	Your Mood
☹ 😕 😐 🙂 ☺	☹ 😕 😐 🙂 ☺

Date

....

Notes for Today

_____
_____
_____
_____
_____
_____
_____
_____
_____

Feeding

_____
_____
_____

Changing

_____
_____
_____

Sleep/Naps

_____
_____
_____

Parent's Day: ☐ Extra crazy! ☐ Survival Mode ☐ OK ☐ Good ☐ Super easy!

Baby's Mood	Your Mood
☹ ☺ ☺ ☺ ☺	☹ ☺ ☺ ☺ ☺

Date

....

Notes for Today

_____
_____
_____
_____
_____
_____
_____
_____
_____

Feeding

_____
_____
_____

Changing

_____
_____
_____

Sleep/Naps

_____
_____
_____

Parent's Day: ☐ Extra crazy! ☐ Survival Mode ☐ OK

☐ Good ☐ Super easy!

Baby's Mood	Your Mood
😣 😖 😐 🙂 😊	😣 😖 😐 🙂 😊

Date

....

Notes for Today

_____
_____
_____
_____
_____
_____
_____
_____
_____
_____

Feeding

_____
_____

Changing

_____
_____

Sleep/Naps

_____
_____

Parent's Day: ☐ Extra crazy! ☐ Survival Mode ☐ OK
☐ Good ☐ Super easy!

Baby's Mood	Your Mood

Date

....

Notes for Today

_____
_____
_____
_____
_____
_____
_____
_____
_____

Feeding

_____
_____
_____

Changing

_____
_____
_____

Sleep/Naps

_____
_____
_____

Parent's Day: ☐ Extra crazy! ☐ Survival Mode ☐ OK

☐ Good ☐ Super easy!

Baby's Mood	Your Mood
☹ 😕 😐 🙂 😊	☹ 😕 😐 🙂 😊

Date

....

Notes for Today

_____
_____
_____
_____
_____
_____
_____
_____

Feeding

_____
_____

Changing

_____
_____

Sleep/Naps

_____
_____

Parent's Day: ☐ Extra crazy! ☐ Survival Mode ☐ OK

☐ Good ☐ Super easy!

Baby's Mood	Your Mood
☹ 😐 😐 🙂 ☺	☹ 😐 😐 🙂 ☺

Date

....

Notes for Today

_____
_____
_____
_____
_____
_____
_____
_____
_____

Feeding

_____
_____

Changing

_____
_____

Sleep/Naps

_____
_____

Parent's Day: ☐ Extra crazy! ☐ Survival Mode ☐ OK
☐ Good ☐ Super easy!

Baby's Mood	Your Mood
😣 😕 😐 🙂 😊	😣 😕 😐 🙂 😊

Date

....

Notes for Today

_____
_____
_____
_____
_____
_____
_____
_____
_____
_____

Feeding

_____
_____

Changing

_____
_____

Sleep/Naps

_____
_____

Parent's Day: ☐ Extra crazy! ☐ Survival Mode ☐ OK
☐ Good ☐ Super easy!

Baby's Mood	Your Mood
😣 😖 😐 🙂 😊	😣 😖 😐 🙂 😊

Date

....

Notes for Today

_____
_____
_____
_____
_____
_____
_____
_____
_____

Feeding

_____
_____

Changing

_____
_____

Sleep/Naps

_____
_____

Parent's Day: ☐ Extra crazy!   ☐ Survival Mode   ☐ OK
☐ Good   ☐ Super easy!

Baby's Mood	Your Mood
☹ 😐 😐 🙂 ☺	☹ 😐 😐 🙂 ☺

Date

....

Notes for Today

_____
_____
_____
_____
_____
_____
_____
_____
_____

Feeding

_____
_____

Changing

_____
_____

Sleep/Naps

_____
_____

Parent's Day: ☐ Extra crazy! ☐ Survival Mode ☐ OK

☐ Good ☐ Super easy!

Baby's Mood	Your Mood
😣 😦 😐 🙂 😊	😣 😦 😐 🙂 😊

Date

....

Notes for Today

_____
_____
_____
_____
_____
_____
_____
_____
_____
_____

Feeding

_____
_____
_____

Changing

_____
_____
_____

Sleep/Naps

_____
_____
_____

Parent's Day: ☐ Extra crazy!   ☐ Survival Mode   ☐ OK

☐ Good   ☐ Super easy!

Baby's Mood	Your Mood
😣 😖 😐 🙂 😊	😣 😖 😐 🙂 😊

Date

....

Notes for Today

_____
_____
_____
_____
_____
_____
_____
_____
_____
_____

Feeding

_____
_____
_____

Changing

_____
_____
_____

Sleep/Naps

_____
_____
_____

Parent's Day: ☐ Extra crazy! ☐ Survival Mode ☐ OK
☐ Good ☐ Super easy!

Baby's Mood	Your Mood
☹ 😐 😐 🙂 😊	☹ 😐 😐 🙂 😊

Date

....

Notes for Today

_____
_____
_____
_____
_____
_____
_____
_____
_____

Feeding

_____
_____

Changing

_____
_____

Sleep/Naps

_____
_____

Parent's Day: ☐ Extra crazy! ☐ Survival Mode ☐ OK
☐ Good ☐ Super easy!

Baby's Mood	Your Mood
😣 😖 😐 🙂 😊	😣 😖 😐 🙂 😊

Date

....

Notes for Today

_____
_____
_____
_____
_____
_____
_____
_____
_____
_____

Feeding

_____
_____

Changing

_____
_____

Sleep/Naps

_____
_____

Parent's Day: ☐ Extra crazy! ☐ Survival Mode ☐ OK

☐ Good ☐ Super easy!

Baby's Mood	Your Mood
😣 😔 😐 🙂 😊	😣 😔 😐 🙂 😊

Date

....

Notes for Today

_____
_____
_____
_____
_____
_____
_____
_____
_____
_____

Feeding

_____
_____
_____

Changing

_____
_____
_____

Sleep/Naps

_____
_____
_____

Parent's Day: ☐ Extra crazy! ☐ Survival Mode ☐ OK
☐ Good ☐ Super easy!

Baby's Mood
☹ 😕 😐 🙂 😊

Your Mood
☹ 😕 😐 🙂 😊

Date

....

Notes for Today

_____
_____
_____
_____
_____
_____
_____
_____
_____
_____
_____

Feeding

_____
_____

Changing

_____
_____

Sleep/Naps

_____
_____

Parent's Day: ☐ Extra crazy! ☐ Survival Mode ☐ OK

☐ Good ☐ Super easy!

Baby's Mood	Your Mood
☹ 😕 😐 🙂 😊	☹ 😕 😐 🙂 😊

Date

....

Notes for Today

_____
_____
_____
_____
_____
_____
_____
_____
_____

Feeding

_____
_____

Changing

_____
_____

Sleep/Naps

_____
_____

Parent's Day: ☐ Extra crazy! ☐ Survival Mode ☐ OK

☐ Good ☐ Super easy!

Baby's Mood	Your Mood
☹ 😐 😐 🙂 😊	☹ 😐 😐 🙂 😊

Date

....

Notes for Today

_____
_____
_____
_____
_____
_____
_____
_____
_____

Feeding

_____
_____
_____

Changing

_____
_____
_____

Sleep/Naps

_____
_____

Parent's Day: ☐ Extra crazy! ☐ Survival Mode ☐ OK

☐ Good ☐ Super easy!

Baby's Mood	Your Mood
☹ ☺	☹ ☺

Date

....

Notes for Today

_____
_____
_____
_____
_____
_____
_____
_____
_____
_____

Feeding

_____
_____

Changing

_____
_____

Sleep/Naps

_____
_____

Parent's Day: ☐ Extra crazy! ☐ Survival Mode ☐ OK
☐ Good ☐ Super easy!

Baby's Mood   Your Mood
☹ 😐 😐 🙂 😊   ☹ 😐 😐 🙂 😊

Date

....

Notes for Today

_____
_____
_____
_____
_____
_____
_____
_____
_____

Feeding
_____
_____

Changing
_____
_____

Sleep/Naps
_____
_____

Parent's Day: ☐ Extra crazy! ☐ Survival Mode ☐ OK

☐ Good ☐ Super easy!

Baby's Mood	Your Mood
☹ 😐 😐 🙂 😊	☹ 😐 😐 🙂 😊

Date

....

Notes for Today

_____
_____
_____
_____
_____
_____
_____
_____
_____

Feeding

_____
_____

Changing

_____
_____

Sleep/Naps

_____
_____

Parent's Day: ☐ Extra crazy! ☐ Survival Mode ☐ OK
               ☐ Good ☐ Super easy!

Baby's Mood	Your Mood
☹ 😕 😐 🙂 ☺	☹ 😕 😐 🙂 ☺

Date

....

Notes for Today

_____
_____
_____
_____
_____
_____
_____
_____
_____

Feeding
_____
_____
_____

Changing
_____
_____
_____

Sleep/Naps
_____
_____
_____

Parent's Day: ☐ Extra crazy! ☐ Survival Mode ☐ OK

☐ Good ☐ Super easy!

Baby's Mood	Your Mood
😣 😩 😐 🙂 😊	😣 😩 😐 🙂 😊

Date

....

Notes for Today

_____
_____
_____
_____
_____
_____
_____
_____
_____

Feeding

_____
_____
_____

Changing

_____
_____
_____

Sleep/Naps

_____
_____
_____

Parent's Day: ☐ Extra crazy!   ☐ Survival Mode   ☐ OK

☐ Good   ☐ Super easy!

Baby's Mood	Your Mood
😣 😐 😐 🙂 😊	😣 😐 😐 🙂 😊

Date

....

Notes for Today

_____
_____
_____
_____
_____
_____
_____
_____
_____
_____

Feeding

_____
_____

Changing

_____
_____

Sleep/Naps

_____
_____

Parent's Day: ☐ Extra crazy! ☐ Survival Mode ☐ OK

☐ Good ☐ Super easy!

Baby's Mood   Your Mood

😣 😖 😐 🙂 😊   😣 😖 😐 🙂 😊

Date

....

Notes for Today

_____
_____
_____
_____
_____
_____
_____
_____
_____

Feeding

_____
_____

Changing

_____
_____

Sleep/Naps

_____
_____

Parent's Day: ☐ Extra crazy! ☐ Survival Mode ☐ OK
☐ Good ☐ Super easy!

Baby's Mood   Your Mood
☹ ☹ ☺ ☺ ☺   ☹ ☹ ☺ ☺ ☺

Date

....

Notes for Today

_____
_____
_____
_____
_____
_____
_____
_____
_____

Feeding

_____
_____
_____

Changing

_____
_____
_____

Sleep/Naps

_____
_____
_____

Parent's Day: ☐ Extra crazy!   ☐ Survival Mode   ☐ OK

☐ Good   ☐ Super easy!

Baby's Mood
☹ 😕 😐 🙂 😊

Your Mood
☹ 😕 😐 🙂 😊

Date

....

Notes for Today

_____
_____
_____
_____
_____
_____
_____
_____
_____

Feeding

_____
_____

Changing

_____
_____

Sleep/Naps

_____
_____

Parent's Day: ☐ Extra crazy!   ☐ Survival Mode   ☐ OK
☐ Good   ☐ Super easy!

Baby's Mood	Your Mood
😝 😕 😐 🙂 😊	😝 😕 😐 🙂 😊

Date

....

Notes for Today

_____
_____
_____
_____
_____
_____
_____
_____
_____

Feeding

_____
_____
_____

Changing

_____
_____
_____

Sleep/Naps

_____
_____
_____

Parent's Day: ☐ Extra crazy! ☐ Survival Mode ☐ OK

☐ Good ☐ Super easy!

Baby's Mood	Your Mood

Date

....

Notes for Today

_____

_____

_____

_____

_____

_____

_____

_____

_____

_____

Feeding

_____

_____

Changing

_____

_____

Sleep/Naps

_____

_____

Parent's Day: ☐ Extra crazy! ☐ Survival Mode ☐ OK

☐ Good ☐ Super easy!

Baby's Mood	Your Mood
☹ 😖 😐 🙂 😊	☹ 😖 😐 🙂 😊

Date

....

Notes for Today

_____
_____
_____
_____
_____
_____
_____
_____
_____

Feeding

_____
_____
_____

Changing

_____
_____
_____

Sleep/Naps

_____
_____
_____

Parent's Day: ☐ Extra crazy! ☐ Survival Mode ☐ OK
             ☐ Good ☐ Super easy!

Baby's Mood	Your Mood

Date

....

Notes for Today

_____
_____
_____
_____
_____
_____
_____
_____
_____

Feeding

_____
_____

Changing

_____
_____

Sleep/Naps

_____
_____

Parent's Day: ☐ Extra crazy! ☐ Survival Mode ☐ OK

☐ Good ☐ Super easy!

Baby's Mood	Your Mood
😣 😖 😐 🙂 😊	😣 😖 😐 🙂 😊

Date

....

Notes for Today

_____
_____
_____
_____
_____
_____
_____
_____
_____

Feeding

_____
_____

Changing

_____
_____

Sleep/Naps

_____
_____

Parent's Day: ☐ Extra crazy! ☐ Survival Mode ☐ OK
☐ Good ☐ Super easy!

Baby's Mood	Your Mood
☹ ☺ ☺ ☺ ☺	☹ ☺ ☺ ☺ ☺

Date

....

Notes for Today

_____
_____
_____
_____
_____
_____
_____
_____
_____

Feeding

_____
_____

Changing

_____
_____

Sleep/Naps

_____
_____

Parent's Day: ☐ Extra crazy! ☐ Survival Mode ☐ OK

☐ Good ☐ Super easy!

Baby's Mood	Your Mood
☹ 😐 😐 🙂 😊	☹ 😐 😐 🙂 😊

Date

....

Notes for Today

_____
_____
_____
_____
_____
_____
_____
_____
_____
_____

Feeding

_____
_____
_____

Changing

_____
_____
_____

Sleep/Naps

_____
_____
_____

Parent's Day: ☐ Extra crazy! ☐ Survival Mode ☐ OK ☐ Good ☐ Super easy!

Baby's Mood	Your Mood
😣 😖 😐 🙂 😊	😣 😖 😐 🙂 😊

Date

....

Notes for Today

_____
_____
_____
_____
_____
_____
_____
_____
_____
_____

Feeding

_____
_____
_____

Changing

_____
_____
_____

Sleep/Naps

_____
_____
_____

Parent's Day: ☐ Extra crazy! ☐ Survival Mode ☐ OK

☐ Good ☐ Super easy!

Baby's Mood	Your Mood
☹ 😐 😐 🙂 😊	☹ 😐 😐 🙂 😊

Date

....

Notes for Today

_____
_____
_____
_____
_____
_____
_____
_____
_____
_____

Feeding

_____
_____

Changing

_____
_____

Sleep/Naps

_____
_____

Parent's Day: ☐ Extra crazy! ☐ Survival Mode ☐ OK

☐ Good ☐ Super easy!

Baby's Mood	Your Mood

Date

....

Notes for Today

_____
_____
_____
_____
_____
_____
_____
_____
_____
_____

Feeding

_____
_____

Changing

_____
_____

Sleep/Naps

_____
_____

Parent's Day: ☐ Extra crazy! ☐ Survival Mode ☐ OK

☐ Good ☐ Super easy!

Baby's Mood	Your Mood
☹ 😐 😐 🙂 😊	☹ 😐 😐 🙂 😊

Date

....

Notes for Today

_____
_____
_____
_____
_____
_____
_____
_____
_____

Feeding

_____
_____
_____

Changing

_____
_____
_____

Sleep/Naps

_____
_____
_____

Parent's Day: ☐ Extra crazy! ☐ Survival Mode ☐ OK

☐ Good ☐ Super easy!

Baby's Mood	Your Mood
☹ ☺ ☺ ☺ ☺	☹ ☺ ☺ ☺ ☺

Date

....

Notes for Today

_____
_____
_____
_____
_____
_____
_____
_____
_____

Feeding

_____
_____
_____

Changing

_____
_____
_____

Sleep/Naps

_____
_____
_____

Parent's Day: ☐ Extra crazy! ☐ Survival Mode ☐ OK

☐ Good ☐ Super easy!

Baby's Mood	Your Mood
😣 😕 😐 🙂 😊	😣 😕 😐 🙂 😊

Date

....

Notes for Today

_____
_____
_____
_____
_____
_____
_____
_____
_____
_____

Feeding

_____
_____

Changing

_____
_____

Sleep/Naps

_____
_____

Parent's Day: ☐ Extra crazy! ☐ Survival Mode ☐ OK

☐ Good ☐ Super easy!

Baby's Mood	Your Mood
☹ 😐 😐 🙂 😊	☹ 😐 😐 🙂 😊

Date

....

Notes for Today

_____
_____
_____
_____
_____
_____
_____
_____
_____

Feeding

_____
_____

Changing

_____
_____

Sleep/Naps

_____
_____

Parent's Day: ☐ Extra crazy! ☐ Survival Mode ☐ OK
☐ Good ☐ Super easy!

Baby's Mood	Your Mood
☹ 😐 😐 🙂 😊	☹ 😐 😐 🙂 😊

Date

....

Notes for Today

_____
_____
_____
_____
_____
_____
_____
_____
_____

Feeding

_____
_____
_____

Changing

_____
_____
_____

Sleep/Naps

_____
_____
_____

Parent's Day: ☐ Extra crazy! ☐ Survival Mode ☐ OK

☐ Good ☐ Super easy!

Baby's Mood	Your Mood
☹ 😦 😐 🙂 😊	☹ 😦 😐 🙂 😊

Date

....

Notes for Today

_____
_____
_____
_____
_____
_____
_____
_____
_____
_____

Feeding
_____
_____
_____

Changing
_____
_____
_____

Sleep/Naps
_____
_____
_____

Parent's Day: ☐ Extra crazy! ☐ Survival Mode ☐ OK

☐ Good ☐ Super easy!

Baby's Mood   Your Mood
😣 😖 😐 🙂 😊   :   😣 😖 😐 🙂 😊

Date

....

Notes for Today

_____

_____

_____

_____

_____

_____

_____

_____

_____

Feeding

_____

_____

Changing

_____

_____

Sleep/Naps

_____

_____

Parent's Day: ☐ Extra crazy! ☐ Survival Mode ☐ OK

☐ Good ☐ Super easy!

Baby's Mood	Your Mood

Date

....

Notes for Today

_____

_____

_____

_____

_____

_____

_____

_____

_____

_____

Feeding

_____

_____

Changing

_____

_____

Sleep/Naps

_____

_____

Parent's Day: ☐ Extra crazy! ☐ Survival Mode ☐ OK

☐ Good ☐ Super easy!

Baby's Mood	Your Mood
☹ 😕 😐 🙂 😊	☹ 😕 😐 🙂 😊

Date

....

Notes for Today

_____
_____
_____
_____
_____
_____
_____
_____
_____

Feeding

_____
_____

Changing

_____
_____
_____

Sleep/Naps

_____
_____

Parent's Day: ☐ Extra crazy! ☐ Survival Mode ☐ OK
☐ Good ☐ Super easy!

Baby's Mood	Your Mood
☹ 😐 😐 🙂 😊	☹ 😐 😐 🙂 😊

Date

....

Notes for Today

_____
_____
_____
_____
_____
_____
_____
_____
_____
_____

Feeding

_____
_____

Changing

_____
_____

Sleep/Naps

_____
_____

Parent's Day: ☐ Extra crazy! ☐ Survival Mode ☐ OK
               ☐ Good   ☐ Super easy!

Baby's Mood	Your Mood
😫 😔 😐 🙂 😊	😫 😔 😐 🙂 😊

Date

....

Notes for Today

_____
_____
_____
_____
_____
_____
_____
_____
_____

Feeding

_____
_____

Changing

_____
_____

Sleep/Naps

_____
_____

Parent's Day: ☐ Extra crazy! ☐ Survival Mode ☐ OK

☐ Good ☐ Super easy!

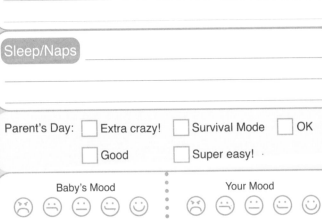

Baby's Mood	Your Mood
😣 😟 😐 🙂 😊	😣 😟 😐 🙂 😊

Date

....

Notes for Today

_____
_____
_____
_____
_____
_____
_____
_____
_____

Feeding

_____
_____

Changing

_____
_____

Sleep/Naps

_____
_____

Parent's Day: ☐ Extra crazy!   ☐ Survival Mode   ☐ OK

☐ Good   ☐ Super easy!

Baby's Mood	Your Mood
☹ 😕 😐 🙂 😊	☹ 😕 😐 🙂 😊

Date

....

Notes for Today

_____
_____
_____
_____
_____
_____
_____
_____
_____

Feeding

_____
_____
_____

Changing

_____
_____
_____

Sleep/Naps

_____
_____
_____

Parent's Day: ☐ Extra crazy! ☐ Survival Mode ☐ OK

☐ Good ☐ Super easy!

Baby's Mood	Your Mood
😣 😕 😐 🙂 😊	😣 😕 😐 🙂 😊

Date

....

Notes for Today

_____

_____

_____

_____

_____

_____

_____

_____

_____

_____

Feeding

_____

_____

_____

Changing

_____

_____

_____

Sleep/Naps

_____

_____

_____

Parent's Day: ☐ Extra crazy! ☐ Survival Mode ☐ OK

☐ Good ☐ Super easy!

Baby's Mood	Your Mood
☹ 😐 😐 🙂 😊	☹ 😐 😐 🙂 😊

Date

....

Notes for Today

_____
_____
_____
_____
_____
_____
_____
_____
_____
_____

Feeding

_____
_____
_____

Changing

_____
_____
_____

Sleep/Naps

_____
_____
_____

Parent's Day: ☐ Extra crazy!   ☐ Survival Mode   ☐ OK
              ☐ Good   ☐ Super easy!

Baby's Mood	Your Mood
☹ ☹ ☺ ☺ ☺	☹ ☹ ☺ ☺ ☺

Date

....

Notes for Today

_____
_____
_____
_____
_____
_____
_____
_____
_____
_____

Feeding

_____
_____

Changing

_____
_____

Sleep/Naps

_____
_____

Parent's Day: ☐ Extra crazy! ☐ Survival Mode ☐ OK
☐ Good ☐ Super easy!

Baby's Mood	Your Mood
☹ 😐 😐 🙂 ☺	☹ 😐 😐 🙂 ☺

Date

....

Notes for Today

_____
_____
_____
_____
_____
_____
_____
_____
_____

Feeding

_____
_____

Changing

_____
_____

Sleep/Naps

_____
_____

Parent's Day: ☐ Extra crazy! ☐ Survival Mode ☐ OK

☐ Good ☐ Super easy!

Baby's Mood	Your Mood
☹ 😕 😐 🙂 😊	☹ 😕 😐 🙂 😊

Date

....

Notes for Today

_____
_____
_____
_____
_____
_____
_____
_____
_____
_____
_____

Feeding

_____
_____
_____

Changing

_____
_____
_____

Sleep/Naps

_____
_____
_____

Parent's Day: ☐ Extra crazy! ☐ Survival Mode ☐ OK

☐ Good ☐ Super easy!

Baby's Mood	Your Mood
😣 😖 😐 🙂 😊	😣 😖 😐 🙂 😊

Date

....

Notes for Today

_____
_____
_____
_____
_____
_____
_____
_____
_____
_____

Feeding

_____
_____
_____

Changing

_____
_____
_____

Sleep/Naps

_____
_____
_____

Parent's Day: ☐ Extra crazy! ☐ Survival Mode ☐ OK

☐ Good ☐ Super easy!

Baby's Mood	Your Mood

Date

....

Notes for Today

_____
_____
_____
_____
_____
_____
_____
_____
_____

Feeding

_____
_____

Changing

_____
_____

Sleep/Naps

_____
_____

Parent's Day: ☐ Extra crazy! ☐ Survival Mode ☐ OK

☐ Good ☐ Super easy!

Baby's Mood ☹ 😐 😐 🙂 😊 : Your Mood ☹ 😐 😐 🙂 😊

Date

···

Notes for Today

_____
_____
_____
_____
_____
_____
_____
_____
_____
_____

Feeding

_____
_____
_____

Changing

_____
_____
_____

Sleep/Naps

_____
_____
_____

Parent's Day: ☐ Extra crazy! ☐ Survival Mode ☐ OK

☐ Good ☐ Super easy!

Baby's Mood	Your Mood
☹ 😐 😐 🙂 😊	☹ 😐 😐 🙂 😊

Date

....

Notes for Today

_____
_____
_____
_____
_____
_____
_____
_____
_____
_____

Feeding

_____
_____
_____

Changing

_____
_____
_____

Sleep/Naps

_____
_____
_____

Parent's Day: ☐ Extra crazy! ☐ Survival Mode ☐ OK

☐ Good ☐ Super easy!

Baby's Mood	Your Mood
☹ 😕 😐 🙂 😊	☹ 😕 😐 🙂 😊

Date

....

Notes for Today

_____
_____
_____
_____
_____
_____
_____
_____
_____

Feeding

_____
_____
_____

Changing

_____
_____
_____

Sleep/Naps

_____
_____
_____

Parent's Day: ☐ Extra crazy! ☐ Survival Mode ☐ OK

☐ Good ☐ Super easy!

Baby's Mood	Your Mood
😣 😑 😐 🙂 😊	😣 😑 😐 🙂 😊

Date

....

Notes for Today

_____
_____
_____
_____
_____
_____
_____
_____
_____
_____

Feeding

_____
_____
_____

Changing

_____
_____
_____

Sleep/Naps

_____
_____
_____

Parent's Day: ☐ Extra crazy! ☐ Survival Mode ☐ OK

☐ Good ☐ Super easy!

Baby's Mood	Your Mood
😣 😕 😐 🙂 😊	😣 😕 😐 🙂 😊

Date

······································

Notes for Today

_____

_____

_____

_____

_____

_____

_____

_____

_____

Feeding

_____

_____

_____

Changing

_____

_____

_____

Sleep/Naps

_____

_____

_____

Parent's Day: ☐ Extra crazy! ☐ Survival Mode ☐ OK

☐ Good ☐ Super easy!

Baby's Mood	Your Mood

Date

....

Notes for Today

(blank lined space)

Feeding

(blank lined space)

Changing

(blank lined space)

Sleep/Naps

(blank lined space)

Parent's Day: ☐ Extra crazy! ☐ Survival Mode ☐ OK
☐ Good ☐ Super easy!

Baby's Mood	Your Mood
😣 😖 😐 🙂 😊	😣 😖 😐 🙂 😊

Date

Notes for Today

_____
_____
_____
_____
_____
_____
_____
_____
_____
_____

Feeding

_____
_____

Changing

_____
_____

Sleep/Naps

_____
_____

Parent's Day: ☐ Extra crazy! ☐ Survival Mode ☐ OK
☐ Good ☐ Super easy!

Baby's Mood

Your Mood

Date

....

Notes for Today

_____
_____
_____
_____
_____
_____
_____
_____
_____

Feeding

_____
_____

Changing

_____
_____

Sleep/Naps

_____
_____

Parent's Day: ☐ Extra crazy! ☐ Survival Mode ☐ OK

☐ Good ☐ Super easy!

Baby's Mood	Your Mood
☹ 😐 😐 🙂 ☺	☹ 😐 😐 🙂 ☺

Date

....

Notes for Today

_____
_____
_____
_____
_____
_____
_____
_____
_____

Feeding
_____
_____
_____

Changing
_____
_____
_____

Sleep/Naps
_____
_____
_____

Parent's Day: ☐ Extra crazy! ☐ Survival Mode ☐ OK

☐ Good ☐ Super easy!

Baby's Mood	Your Mood
☹ 😕 😐 🙂 😊	☹ 😕 😐 🙂 😊

Date

....

Notes for Today

_____
_____
_____
_____
_____
_____
_____
_____
_____

Feeding

_____
_____

Changing

_____
_____

Sleep/Naps

_____
_____

Parent's Day: ☐ Extra crazy! ☐ Survival Mode ☐ OK

☐ Good ☐ Super easy!

Baby's Mood	Your Mood
☹ 😕 😐 🙂 😊	☹ 😕 😐 🙂 😊

Date

....

Notes for Today

_____
_____
_____
_____
_____
_____
_____
_____
_____
_____

Feeding

_____
_____

Changing

_____
_____

Sleep/Naps

_____
_____

Parent's Day: ☐ Extra crazy! ☐ Survival Mode ☐ OK

☐ Good ☐ Super easy!

Baby's Mood	Your Mood
☹ 😖 😐 🙂 😊	☹ 😖 😐 🙂 😊

Date

....

Notes for Today

_____
_____
_____
_____
_____
_____
_____
_____
_____

Feeding

_____
_____

Changing

_____
_____

Sleep/Naps

_____
_____

Parent's Day: ☐ Extra crazy! ☐ Survival Mode ☐ OK

☐ Good ☐ Super easy!

Baby's Mood	Your Mood
☹ 😐 😐 🙂 😊	☹ 😐 😐 🙂 😊

Date

....

Notes for Today

_____
_____
_____
_____
_____
_____
_____
_____

Feeding

_____
_____

Changing

_____
_____
_____

Sleep/Naps

_____
_____

Parent's Day: ☐ Extra crazy! ☐ Survival Mode ☐ OK

☐ Good ☐ Super easy!

Baby's Mood	Your Mood
☹ 😕 😐 🙂 😊	☹ 😕 😐 🙂 😊

Date

....

Notes for Today

_____
_____
_____
_____
_____
_____
_____
_____
_____
_____
_____

Feeding

_____
_____

Changing

_____
_____

Sleep/Naps

_____
_____

Parent's Day: ☐ Extra crazy! ☐ Survival Mode ☐ OK
☐ Good ☐ Super easy!

Baby's Mood	Your Mood
☹ 😕 😐 🙂 😊	☹ 😕 😐 🙂 😊

Date

....

Notes for Today

_____
_____
_____
_____
_____
_____
_____
_____
_____
_____

Feeding

_____
_____
_____

Changing

_____
_____
_____

Sleep/Naps

_____
_____
_____

Parent's Day: ☐ Extra crazy! ☐ Survival Mode ☐ OK

☐ Good ☐ Super easy!

Baby's Mood ☹ 😕 😐 🙂 😊 : Your Mood ☹ 😕 😐 🙂 😊

Date

....

Notes for Today

_____
_____
_____
_____
_____
_____
_____
_____
_____

Feeding

_____
_____

Changing

_____
_____

Sleep/Naps

_____
_____

Parent's Day: ☐ Extra crazy! ☐ Survival Mode ☐ OK

☐ Good ☐ Super easy!

Baby's Mood	Your Mood
☹ 😐 😐 🙂 😊	☹ 😐 😐 🙂 😊

Date

....

Notes for Today

_____
_____
_____
_____
_____
_____
_____
_____
_____

Feeding

_____
_____

Changing

_____
_____

Sleep/Naps

_____
_____

Parent's Day: ☐ Extra crazy! ☐ Survival Mode ☐ OK

☐ Good ☐ Super easy!

Baby's Mood   Your Mood

☹ 😐 😐 🙂 😊   ☹ 😐 😐 🙂 😊

Date

....

Notes for Today

_____
_____
_____
_____
_____
_____
_____
_____
_____
_____

Feeding

_____
_____

Changing

_____
_____

Sleep/Naps

_____
_____

Parent's Day: ☐ Extra crazy! ☐ Survival Mode ☐ OK

☐ Good ☐ Super easy!

Baby's Mood	Your Mood
😫 😔 😐 🙂 😊	😫 😔 😐 🙂 😊

Date

....

Notes for Today

_____

_____

_____

_____

_____

_____

_____

_____

_____

Feeding

_____

_____

Changing

_____

_____

Sleep/Naps

_____

_____

Parent's Day: ☐ Extra crazy! ☐ Survival Mode ☐ OK

☐ Good ☐ Super easy!

Baby's Mood	Your Mood
☹ 😐 😐 🙂 😊	☹ 😐 😐 🙂 😊

Date

....

Notes for Today

_____

_____

_____

_____

_____

_____

_____

_____

_____

_____

Feeding

_____

_____

Changing

_____

_____

Sleep/Naps

_____

_____

Parent's Day: ☐ Extra crazy! ☐ Survival Mode ☐ OK

☐ Good ☐ Super easy!

Baby's Mood	Your Mood
😫 😕 😐 🙂 😊	😫 😕 😐 🙂 😊

Date

....

Notes for Today

_____
_____
_____
_____
_____
_____
_____
_____
_____
_____

Feeding

_____
_____
_____

Changing

_____
_____
_____

Sleep/Naps

_____
_____

Parent's Day: ☐ Extra crazy! ☐ Survival Mode ☐ OK

☐ Good ☐ Super easy!

Baby's Mood	Your Mood
☹ 😐 😐 🙂 😊	☹ 😐 😐 🙂 😊

Date

....

Notes for Today

_____
_____
_____
_____
_____
_____
_____
_____
_____
_____

Feeding

_____
_____
_____

Changing

_____
_____
_____

Sleep/Naps

_____
_____
_____

Parent's Day: ☐ Extra crazy! ☐ Survival Mode ☐ OK
☐ Good ☐ Super easy!

Baby's Mood   Your Mood
☹ ☹ ☺ ☺ ☺   ☹ ☹ ☺ ☺ ☺

Date

....

Notes for Today

_____
_____
_____
_____
_____
_____
_____
_____
_____

Feeding

_____
_____

Changing

_____
_____

Sleep/Naps

_____
_____

Parent's Day: ☐ Extra crazy! ☐ Survival Mode ☐ OK

☐ Good ☐ Super easy!

Baby's Mood	Your Mood
☹ 😐 😐 🙂 😊	☹ 😐 😐 🙂 😊

Date

....

Notes for Today

_____
_____
_____
_____
_____
_____
_____
_____
_____

Feeding

_____
_____

Changing

_____
_____

Sleep/Naps

_____
_____

Parent's Day: ☐ Extra crazy! ☐ Survival Mode ☐ OK
☐ Good ☐ Super easy!

Baby's Mood   Your Mood
☹ 😕 😐 🙂 😊   ☹ 😕 😐 🙂 😊

Date

....

Notes for Today

_____
_____
_____
_____
_____
_____
_____
_____
_____

Feeding

_____
_____
_____

Changing

_____
_____
_____

Sleep/Naps

_____
_____
_____

Parent's Day: ☐ Extra crazy! ☐ Survival Mode ☐ OK

☐ Good ☐ Super easy!

Baby's Mood   Your Mood

😣 😕 😐 🙂 😊   :   😣 😕 😐 🙂 😊

Date

....

Notes for Today

_____
_____
_____
_____
_____
_____
_____
_____
_____
_____

Feeding

_____
_____
_____

Changing

_____
_____
_____

Sleep/Naps

_____
_____
_____

Parent's Day: ☐ Extra crazy! ☐ Survival Mode ☐ OK
☐ Good ☐ Super easy!

Baby's Mood	Your Mood
☹ 😐 😐 🙂 😊	☹ 😐 😐 🙂 😊

Date

....

Notes for Today

_____

_____

_____

_____

_____

_____

_____

_____

_____

_____

Feeding

_____

_____

Changing

_____

_____

Sleep/Naps

_____

_____

Parent's Day: ☐ Extra crazy! ☐ Survival Mode ☐ OK
☐ Good ☐ Super easy!

Baby's Mood

Your Mood

Date

....

Notes for Today

_____
_____
_____
_____
_____
_____
_____
_____
_____

Feeding

_____
_____

Changing

_____
_____

Sleep/Naps

_____
_____

Parent's Day: ☐ Extra crazy! ☐ Survival Mode ☐ OK

☐ Good ☐ Super easy!

Baby's Mood	Your Mood
☹ 😐 😐 🙂 😊	☹ 😐 😐 🙂 😊

Date

....

Notes for Today

_____
_____
_____
_____
_____
_____
_____
_____
_____

Feeding

_____
_____

Changing

_____
_____
_____

Sleep/Naps

_____
_____
_____

Parent's Day: ☐ Extra crazy!   ☐ Survival Mode   ☐ OK

☐ Good   ☐ Super easy!

Baby's Mood   Your Mood
☹ ☹ 😐 🙂 😊   ☹ ☹ 😐 🙂 😊

Date

....

Notes for Today

_____
_____
_____
_____
_____
_____
_____
_____
_____
_____

Feeding

_____
_____

Changing

_____
_____

Sleep/Naps

_____
_____

Parent's Day: ☐ Extra crazy! ☐ Survival Mode ☐ OK

☐ Good ☐ Super easy!

Baby's Mood	Your Mood
☹ 😐 😐 🙂 😊	☹ 😐 😐 🙂 😊

Date

....

Notes for Today

_____
_____
_____
_____
_____
_____
_____
_____
_____

Feeding

_____
_____

Changing

_____
_____

Sleep/Naps

_____
_____

Parent's Day: ☐ Extra crazy! ☐ Survival Mode ☐ OK
☐ Good ☐ Super easy!

Baby's Mood	Your Mood

Date

....

Notes for Today

_____
_____
_____
_____
_____
_____
_____
_____
_____

Feeding

_____
_____

Changing

_____
_____

Sleep/Naps

_____
_____

Parent's Day: ☐ Extra crazy! ☐ Survival Mode ☐ OK

☐ Good ☐ Super easy!

Baby's Mood	Your Mood
☹ 😐 😐 🙂 😊	☹ 😐 😐 🙂 😊

Date

....

Notes for Today

_____
_____
_____
_____
_____
_____
_____
_____

Feeding

_____
_____
_____

Changing

_____
_____
_____

Sleep/Naps

_____
_____
_____

Parent's Day: ☐ Extra crazy! ☐ Survival Mode ☐ OK

☐ Good ☐ Super easy!

Baby's Mood	Your Mood
😣 😖 😐 🙂 😊	😣 😖 😐 🙂 😊

Date

....

Notes for Today

_____
_____
_____
_____
_____
_____
_____
_____
_____
_____

Feeding

_____
_____
_____

Changing

_____
_____
_____

Sleep/Naps

_____
_____
_____

Parent's Day: ☐ Extra crazy! ☐ Survival Mode ☐ OK ☐ Good ☐ Super easy!

Baby's Mood	Your Mood
😣 😖 😐 🙂 😊	😣 😖 😐 🙂 😊

Date

....

Notes for Today

_____
_____
_____
_____
_____
_____
_____
_____
_____
_____

Feeding

_____
_____
_____

Changing

_____
_____
_____

Sleep/Naps

_____
_____
_____

Parent's Day: ☐ Extra crazy! ☐ Survival Mode ☐ OK
☐ Good ☐ Super easy!

Baby's Mood	Your Mood
😖 😕 😐 🙂 😊	😖 😕 😐 🙂 😊

Date

....

Notes for Today

_____
_____
_____
_____
_____
_____
_____
_____
_____

Feeding

_____
_____

Changing

_____
_____

Sleep/Naps

_____
_____

Parent's Day: ☐ Extra crazy! ☐ Survival Mode ☐ OK
☐ Good ☐ Super easy!

Baby's Mood	Your Mood
😣 😖 😐 🙂 😊	😣 😖 😐 🙂 😊

Date

....

Notes for Today

_____
_____
_____
_____
_____
_____
_____
_____
_____

Feeding

_____
_____
_____

Changing

_____
_____
_____

Sleep/Naps

_____
_____
_____

Parent's Day: ☐ Extra crazy! ☐ Survival Mode ☐ OK
☐ Good ☐ Super easy!

Baby's Mood
😣 😑 😐 🙂 😊

Your Mood
😣 😑 😐 🙂 😊

Date

....

Notes for Today

_____
_____
_____
_____
_____
_____
_____
_____
_____
_____

Feeding

_____
_____
_____

Changing

_____
_____
_____

Sleep/Naps

_____
_____
_____

Parent's Day: ☐ Extra crazy! ☐ Survival Mode ☐ OK

☐ Good ☐ Super easy!

Baby's Mood	Your Mood
😣 😕 😐 🙂 😊	😣 😕 😐 🙂 😊

Date

....

Notes for Today

_____
_____
_____
_____
_____
_____
_____
_____
_____
_____

Feeding

_____
_____

Changing

_____
_____

Sleep/Naps

_____
_____

Parent's Day: ☐ Extra crazy! ☐ Survival Mode ☐ OK

☐ Good ☐ Super easy!

Baby's Mood	Your Mood
😣 😕 😐 🙂 😊	😣 😕 😐 🙂 😊

Date

....

Notes for Today

_____
_____
_____
_____
_____
_____
_____
_____
_____
_____

Feeding

_____
_____
_____

Changing

_____
_____
_____

Sleep/Naps

_____
_____
_____

Parent's Day: ☐ Extra crazy!   ☐ Survival Mode   ☐ OK

☐ Good   ☐ Super easy!

Baby's Mood	Your Mood
☹ 😐 😐 🙂 😊	☹ 😐 😐 🙂 😊

Date

....

Notes for Today

_____
_____
_____
_____
_____
_____
_____
_____
_____

Feeding

_____
_____

Changing

_____
_____
_____

Sleep/Naps

_____
_____

Parent's Day: ☐ Extra crazy! ☐ Survival Mode ☐ OK

☐ Good ☐ Super easy!

Baby's Mood	Your Mood
☹ 😐 😐 🙂 ☺	☹ 😐 😐 🙂 ☺

Date

....

Notes for Today

_____

_____

_____

_____

_____

_____

_____

_____

Feeding

_____

_____

Changing

_____

_____

Sleep/Naps

_____

_____

Parent's Day: ☐ Extra crazy! ☐ Survival Mode ☐ OK

☐ Good ☐ Super easy!

Baby's Mood	Your Mood
😣 😑 😐 🙂 😊	😣 😑 😐 🙂 😊

Date

....

Notes for Today

_____
_____
_____
_____
_____
_____
_____
_____
_____

Feeding

_____
_____

Changing

_____
_____

Sleep/Naps

_____
_____

Parent's Day: ☐ Extra crazy! ☐ Survival Mode ☐ OK

☐ Good ☐ Super easy!

Baby's Mood	Your Mood

Date

....

Notes for Today

_____
_____
_____
_____
_____
_____
_____
_____
_____

Feeding

_____
_____
_____

Changing

_____
_____
_____

Sleep/Naps

_____
_____
_____

Parent's Day: ☐ Extra crazy! ☐ Survival Mode ☐ OK

☐ Good ☐ Super easy!

Baby's Mood	Your Mood
☹ 😐 😐 🙂 😊	☹ 😐 😐 🙂 😊

Date

....

Notes for Today

_____
_____
_____
_____
_____
_____
_____
_____
_____

Feeding

_____
_____
_____

Changing

_____
_____
_____

Sleep/Naps

_____
_____

Parent's Day: ☐ Extra crazy! ☐ Survival Mode ☐ OK

☐ Good ☐ Super easy!

Baby's Mood	Your Mood
☹ 😐 😐 🙂 😊	☹ 😐 😐 🙂 😊

Date

....

Notes for Today

_____
_____
_____
_____
_____
_____
_____
_____
_____

Feeding

_____
_____

Changing

_____
_____

Sleep/Naps

_____
_____

Parent's Day: ☐ Extra crazy! ☐ Survival Mode ☐ OK
☐ Good ☐ Super easy!

Baby's Mood	Your Mood
😣 😖 😐 🙂 😊	😣 😖 😐 🙂 😊

Date

....

Notes for Today

_____
_____
_____
_____
_____
_____
_____
_____
_____
_____

Feeding

_____
_____

Changing

_____
_____

Sleep/Naps

_____
_____

Parent's Day: ☐ Extra crazy! ☐ Survival Mode ☐ OK

☐ Good ☐ Super easy!

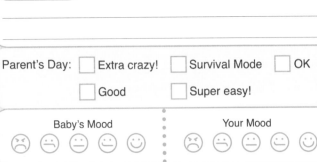

Baby's Mood	Your Mood
☹ 😕 😐 🙂 😊	☹ 😕 😐 🙂 😊

Date

....

Notes for Today

_____
_____
_____
_____
_____
_____
_____
_____
_____

Feeding

_____
_____

Changing

_____
_____

Sleep/Naps

_____
_____

Parent's Day: ☐ Extra crazy! ☐ Survival Mode ☐ OK
☐ Good ☐ Super easy!

Baby's Mood	Your Mood
☹ 😐 😐 🙂 ☺	☹ 😐 😐 🙂 ☺

Date

....

Notes for Today

_____
_____
_____
_____
_____
_____
_____
_____
_____

Feeding

_____
_____

Changing

_____
_____
_____

Sleep/Naps

_____
_____

Parent's Day: ☐ Extra crazy!   ☐ Survival Mode   ☐ OK

☐ Good   ☐ Super easy!

Baby's Mood	Your Mood
😣 😕 😐 🙂 😊	😣 😕 😐 🙂 😊

Date

....

Notes for Today

_____
_____
_____
_____
_____
_____
_____
_____
_____

Feeding

_____
_____
_____

Changing

_____
_____
_____

Sleep/Naps

_____
_____
_____

Parent's Day: ☐ Extra crazy! ☐ Survival Mode ☐ OK

☐ Good ☐ Super easy!

Baby's Mood	Your Mood
☹ 😕 😐 🙂 😊	☹ 😕 😐 🙂 😊

Date

....

Notes for Today

_____
_____
_____
_____
_____
_____
_____
_____
_____
_____

Feeding

_____
_____

Changing

_____
_____

Sleep/Naps

_____
_____

Parent's Day: ☐ Extra crazy! ☐ Survival Mode ☐ OK

☐ Good ☐ Super easy!

Baby's Mood	Your Mood
😣 😔 😐 🙂 😊	😣 😔 😐 🙂 😊

Date

....

Notes for Today

_____
_____
_____
_____
_____
_____
_____
_____
_____
_____

Feeding

_____
_____
_____

Changing

_____
_____
_____

Sleep/Naps

_____
_____
_____

Parent's Day: ☐ Extra crazy! ☐ Survival Mode ☐ OK

☐ Good ☐ Super easy!

Baby's Mood	Your Mood
😣 😑 😐 🙂 😊	😣 😑 😐 🙂 😊

Date

....

Notes for Today

_____
_____
_____
_____
_____
_____
_____
_____
_____

Feeding

_____
_____

Changing

_____
_____

Sleep/Naps

_____
_____

Parent's Day: ☐ Extra crazy! ☐ Survival Mode ☐ OK

☐ Good ☐ Super easy!

Baby's Mood	Your Mood
☹ ☹ ☺ ☺ ☺	☹ ☹ ☺ ☺ ☺

Date

....

Notes for Today

_____
_____
_____
_____
_____
_____
_____
_____
_____
_____

Feeding

_____
_____
_____

Changing

_____
_____
_____

Sleep/Naps

_____
_____
_____

Parent's Day: ☐ Extra crazy! ☐ Survival Mode ☐ OK

☐ Good ☐ Super easy!

Baby's Mood	Your Mood
☹ 😕 😐 🙂 😊	☹ 😕 😐 🙂 😊

Date

....

Notes for Today

_____
_____
_____
_____
_____
_____
_____
_____
_____
_____

Feeding

_____
_____

Changing

_____
_____

Sleep/Naps

_____
_____

Parent's Day: ☐ Extra crazy! ☐ Survival Mode ☐ OK

☐ Good ☐ Super easy!

Baby's Mood	Your Mood
😣 😐 😐 😊 ☺	😣 😐 😐 😊 ☺

Date

....

Notes for Today

_____
_____
_____
_____
_____
_____
_____
_____
_____

Feeding

_____
_____

Changing

_____
_____

Sleep/Naps

_____
_____

Parent's Day: ☐ Extra crazy! ☐ Survival Mode ☐ OK

☐ Good ☐ Super easy!

Baby's Mood | Your Mood
☹ 🙁 😐 🙂 😊 | ☹ 🙁 😐 🙂 😊

Date

....

Notes for Today

_____
_____
_____
_____
_____
_____
_____
_____
_____

Feeding

_____
_____

Changing

_____
_____
_____

Sleep/Naps

_____
_____
_____

Parent's Day: ☐ Extra crazy! ☐ Survival Mode ☐ OK

☐ Good ☐ Super easy!

Baby's Mood   Your Mood

☹ ☹ ☺ ☺ ☺   ☹ ☹ ☺ ☺ ☺

Date

....

Notes for Today

_____
_____
_____
_____
_____
_____
_____
_____
_____

Feeding

_____
_____
_____

Changing

_____
_____
_____

Sleep/Naps

_____
_____
_____

Parent's Day: ☐ Extra crazy! ☐ Survival Mode ☐ OK

☐ Good ☐ Super easy!

Baby's Mood	Your Mood
😣 😔 😐 🙂 😊	😣 😔 😐 🙂 😊

Date

....

Notes for Today

_____
_____
_____
_____
_____
_____
_____
_____
_____

Feeding

_____
_____

Changing

_____
_____

Sleep/Naps

_____
_____

Parent's Day: ☐ Extra crazy! ☐ Survival Mode ☐ OK
☐ Good ☐ Super easy!

Baby's Mood	Your Mood
☹ 😐 😐 🙂 😊	☹ 😐 😐 🙂 😊

Date

....

Notes for Today

_____
_____
_____
_____
_____
_____
_____
_____
_____

Feeding

_____
_____

Changing

_____
_____

Sleep/Naps

_____
_____

Parent's Day: ☐ Extra crazy! ☐ Survival Mode ☐ OK
☐ Good ☐ Super easy!

Baby's Mood	Your Mood
☹ 🙁 😐 🙂 ☺	☹ 🙁 😐 🙂 ☺

Date

....

Notes for Today

_____
_____
_____
_____
_____
_____
_____
_____
_____

Feeding

_____
_____

Changing

_____
_____
_____

Sleep/Naps

_____
_____
_____

Parent's Day: ☐ Extra crazy! ☐ Survival Mode ☐ OK
☐ Good ☐ Super easy!

Baby's Mood	Your Mood
☹ 😖 😐 🙂 😊	☹ 😖 😐 🙂 😊

Date

....

Notes for Today

_____
_____
_____
_____
_____
_____
_____
_____
_____

Feeding

_____
_____
_____

Changing

_____
_____
_____

Sleep/Naps

_____
_____
_____

Parent's Day: ☐ Extra crazy! ☐ Survival Mode ☐ OK
☐ Good ☐ Super easy!

Baby's Mood	Your Mood
☹ 😕 😐 🙂 😊	☹ 😕 😐 🙂 😊

Date

....

Notes for Today

_____

_____

_____

_____

_____

_____

_____

_____

_____

_____

Feeding

_____

_____

Changing

_____

_____

Sleep/Naps

_____

_____

Parent's Day: ☐ Extra crazy! ☐ Survival Mode ☐ OK

☐ Good ☐ Super easy!

Baby's Mood

☹ 😐 😐 🙂 😊

Your Mood

☹ 😐 😐 🙂 😊

Date

....

Notes for Today

_____

_____

_____

_____

_____

_____

_____

_____

_____

Feeding

_____

_____

Changing

_____

_____

Sleep/Naps

_____

_____

Parent's Day: ☐ Extra crazy! ☐ Survival Mode ☐ OK

☐ Good ☐ Super easy!

Baby's Mood	Your Mood
☹ 😐 😐 🙂 😊	☹ 😐 😐 🙂 😊

Date

....

Notes for Today

_____
_____
_____
_____
_____
_____
_____
_____
_____
_____

Feeding

_____
_____
_____

Changing

_____
_____
_____

Sleep/Naps

_____
_____
_____

Parent's Day: ☐ Extra crazy! ☐ Survival Mode ☐ OK

☐ Good ☐ Super easy!

Baby's Mood	Your Mood
☹ 😐 😐 🙂 😊	☹ 😐 😐 🙂 😊

Date

....

Notes for Today

_____
_____
_____
_____
_____
_____
_____
_____
_____
_____

Feeding

_____
_____

Changing

_____
_____

Sleep/Naps

_____
_____

Parent's Day: ☐ Extra crazy! ☐ Survival Mode ☐ OK
☐ Good ☐ Super easy!

Baby's Mood	Your Mood
☹ 😕 😐 🙂 😊	☹ 😕 😐 🙂 😊

Date

....

Notes for Today

_____
_____
_____
_____
_____
_____
_____
_____
_____
_____

Feeding

_____
_____

Changing

_____
_____

Sleep/Naps

_____
_____

Parent's Day: ☐ Extra crazy! ☐ Survival Mode ☐ OK
☐ Good ☐ Super easy!

Baby's Mood	Your Mood
☹ 😐 😐 🙂 😊	☹ 😐 😐 🙂 😊

Date

....

Notes for Today

_____
_____
_____
_____
_____
_____
_____
_____
_____
_____

Feeding

_____
_____

Changing

_____
_____

Sleep/Naps

_____
_____

Parent's Day: ☐ Extra crazy! ☐ Survival Mode ☐ OK

☐ Good ☐ Super easy!

Baby's Mood	Your Mood

Date

....

Notes for Today

_____

_____

_____

_____

_____

_____

_____

_____

_____

Feeding

_____

_____

Changing

_____

_____

Sleep/Naps

_____

_____

Parent's Day: ☐ Extra crazy! ☐ Survival Mode ☐ OK

☐ Good ☐ Super easy!

Baby's Mood	Your Mood
😣 😖 😐 🙂 😊	😣 😖 😐 🙂 😊

Date

....

Notes for Today

_____
_____
_____
_____
_____
_____
_____
_____
_____

Feeding

_____
_____
_____

Changing

_____
_____
_____

Sleep/Naps

_____
_____
_____

Parent's Day: ☐ Extra crazy! ☐ Survival Mode ☐ OK
☐ Good ☐ Super easy!

Baby's Mood
☹ ☹ 😐 🙂 😊

Your Mood
☹ ☹ 😐 🙂 😊

Date

....

Notes for Today

_____
_____
_____
_____
_____
_____
_____
_____
_____

Feeding
_____
_____

Changing
_____
_____

Sleep/Naps
_____
_____

Parent's Day: ☐ Extra crazy! ☐ Survival Mode ☐ OK
☐ Good ☐ Super easy!

Baby's Mood	Your Mood
	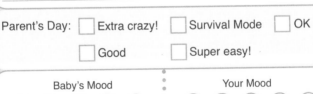

Date

....

Notes for Today

_____
_____
_____
_____
_____
_____
_____
_____
_____

Feeding

_____
_____

Changing

_____
_____

Sleep/Naps

_____
_____

Parent's Day: ☐ Extra crazy! ☐ Survival Mode ☐ OK
               ☐ Good   ☐ Super easy!

Baby's Mood	Your Mood
☹ 😐 😐 🙂 😊	☹ 😐 😐 🙂 😊

Date

....

Notes for Today

_____
_____
_____
_____
_____
_____
_____
_____
_____
_____

Feeding

_____
_____

Changing

_____
_____

Sleep/Naps

_____
_____

Parent's Day: ☐ Extra crazy! ☐ Survival Mode ☐ OK

☐ Good ☐ Super easy!

Baby's Mood	Your Mood
😖 😕 😐 🙂 😊	😖 😕 😐 🙂 😊

Date

....

Notes for Today

_____
_____
_____
_____
_____
_____
_____
_____
_____
_____

Feeding

_____
_____

Changing

_____
_____

Sleep/Naps

_____
_____

Parent's Day: ☐ Extra crazy! ☐ Survival Mode ☐ OK
☐ Good ☐ Super easy!

Baby's Mood	Your Mood
😣 😕 😐 🙂 😊	😣 😕 😐 🙂 😊

Date

....

Notes for Today

_____
_____
_____
_____
_____
_____
_____
_____
_____

Feeding

_____
_____

Changing

_____
_____

Sleep/Naps

_____
_____

Parent's Day: ☐ Extra crazy! ☐ Survival Mode ☐ OK

☐ Good ☐ Super easy!

Baby's Mood ☹ ☺ ☺ ☺ ☺ : Your Mood ☹ ☺ ☺ ☺ ☺

Date

....

Notes for Today

_____
_____
_____
_____
_____
_____
_____
_____
_____

Feeding

_____
_____

Changing

_____
_____

Sleep/Naps

_____
_____

Parent's Day: ☐ Extra crazy! ☐ Survival Mode ☐ OK

☐ Good ☐ Super easy!

Baby's Mood	Your Mood
☹ 😐 😐 🙂 ☺	☹ 😐 😐 🙂 ☺

Date

....

Notes for Today

_____
_____
_____
_____
_____
_____
_____
_____
_____

Feeding

_____
_____
_____

Changing

_____
_____
_____

Sleep/Naps

_____
_____

Parent's Day: ☐ Extra crazy! ☐ Survival Mode ☐ OK

☐ Good ☐ Super easy!

Baby's Mood   Your Mood

☹ 😐 😐 🙂 😊 : ☹ 😐 😐 🙂 😊

Date

....

Notes for Today

_____
_____
_____
_____
_____
_____
_____
_____
_____
_____

Feeding

_____
_____
_____

Changing

_____
_____
_____

Sleep/Naps

_____
_____
_____

Parent's Day: ☐ Extra crazy! ☐ Survival Mode ☐ OK

☐ Good ☐ Super easy!

Baby's Mood	Your Mood
😣 😕 😐 🙂 😊	😣 😕 😐 🙂 😊

Date

....

Notes for Today

_____
_____
_____
_____
_____
_____
_____
_____
_____

Feeding

_____
_____

Changing

_____
_____

Sleep/Naps

_____
_____

Parent's Day: ☐ Extra crazy! ☐ Survival Mode ☐ OK

☐ Good ☐ Super easy!

Baby's Mood	Your Mood
☹ ☹ ☺ ☺ ☺	☹ ☹ ☺ ☺ ☺

Date

....

Notes for Today

_____
_____
_____
_____
_____
_____
_____
_____
_____
_____

Feeding

_____
_____

Changing

_____
_____

Sleep/Naps

_____
_____

Parent's Day: ☐ Extra crazy! ☐ Survival Mode ☐ OK

☐ Good ☐ Super easy!

Baby's Mood   Your Mood
😣 😖 😐 🙂 😊   :   😣 😖 😐 🙂 😊

Date

....

Notes for Today

_____
_____
_____
_____
_____
_____
_____
_____
_____

Feeding
_____
_____
_____

Changing
_____
_____
_____

Sleep/Naps
_____
_____
_____

Parent's Day: ☐ Extra crazy!   ☐ Survival Mode   ☐ OK
              ☐ Good   ☐ Super easy!

Baby's Mood   Your Mood
☹ 😐 😐 🙂 ☺   ☹ 😐 😐 🙂 ☺

Date

....

Notes for Today

_____
_____
_____
_____
_____
_____
_____
_____
_____
_____

Feeding

_____
_____

Changing

_____
_____

Sleep/Naps

_____
_____

Parent's Day: ☐ Extra crazy! ☐ Survival Mode ☐ OK
☐ Good ☐ Super easy!

Baby's Mood	Your Mood
😣 😕 😐 🙂 😊	😣 😕 😐 🙂 😊

Date

....

Notes for Today

_____
_____
_____
_____
_____
_____
_____
_____
_____
_____

Feeding

_____
_____
_____

Changing

_____
_____
_____

Sleep/Naps

_____
_____
_____

Parent's Day: ☐ Extra crazy!   ☐ Survival Mode   ☐ OK
               ☐ Good   ☐ Super easy!

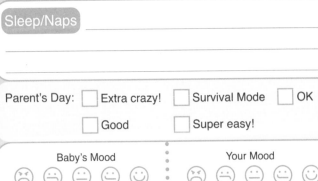

Baby's Mood	Your Mood
☹ ☺ ☺ ☺ ☺	☹ ☺ ☺ ☺ ☺

Date

....

Notes for Today

_____
_____
_____
_____
_____
_____
_____
_____
_____
_____

Feeding

_____
_____

Changing

_____
_____

Sleep/Naps

_____
_____

Parent's Day: ☐ Extra crazy! ☐ Survival Mode ☐ OK

☐ Good ☐ Super easy!

Baby's Mood	Your Mood

Date

....

Notes for Today

_____
_____
_____
_____
_____
_____
_____
_____
_____
_____

Feeding

_____
_____
_____

Changing

_____
_____
_____

Sleep/Naps

_____
_____
_____

Parent's Day: ☐ Extra crazy! ☐ Survival Mode ☐ OK
              ☐ Good ☐ Super easy!

Baby's Mood	Your Mood

Date

....

Notes for Today

_____
_____
_____
_____
_____
_____
_____
_____
_____
_____

Feeding

_____
_____

Changing

_____
_____

Sleep/Naps

_____
_____

Parent's Day: ☐ Extra crazy! ☐ Survival Mode ☐ OK

☐ Good ☐ Super easy!

Baby's Mood	Your Mood
☹ 😕 😐 🙂 😊	☹ 😕 😐 🙂 😊

Date

....

Notes for Today

_____
_____
_____
_____
_____
_____
_____
_____
_____

Feeding

_____
_____

Changing

_____
_____

Sleep/Naps

_____
_____

Parent's Day: ☐ Extra crazy! ☐ Survival Mode ☐ OK
☐ Good ☐ Super easy!

Baby's Mood	Your Mood
😣 😔 😐 🙂 😊	😣 😔 😐 🙂 😊

Date

....

Notes for Today

_____
_____
_____
_____
_____
_____
_____
_____
_____
_____

Feeding

_____
_____
_____

Changing

_____
_____
_____

Sleep/Naps

_____
_____
_____

Parent's Day: ☐ Extra crazy! ☐ Survival Mode ☐ OK

☐ Good ☐ Super easy!

Baby's Mood	Your Mood
☹ 😐 😐 🙂 😊	☹ 😐 😐 🙂 😊

Date

....

Notes for Today

_____
_____
_____
_____
_____
_____
_____
_____
_____

Feeding

_____
_____
_____

Changing

_____
_____
_____

Sleep/Naps

_____
_____
_____

Parent's Day: ☐ Extra crazy! ☐ Survival Mode ☐ OK

☐ Good ☐ Super easy!

Baby's Mood   Your Mood

☹ 🙁 😐 🙂 😊   ☹ 🙁 😐 🙂 😊

Date

....

Notes for Today

_____
_____
_____
_____
_____
_____
_____
_____
_____
_____

Feeding

_____
_____
_____

Changing

_____
_____
_____

Sleep/Naps

_____
_____

Parent's Day: ☐ Extra crazy! ☐ Survival Mode ☐ OK
☐ Good ☐ Super easy!

Baby's Mood   Your Mood
☹ ☹ ☺ ☺ ☺   ☹ ☹ ☺ ☺ ☺

Date

....

Notes for Today

_____
_____
_____
_____
_____
_____
_____
_____
_____

Feeding

_____
_____

Changing

_____
_____

Sleep/Naps

_____
_____

Parent's Day: ☐ Extra crazy! ☐ Survival Mode ☐ OK

☐ Good ☐ Super easy!

Baby's Mood	Your Mood
😖 😣 😐 🙂 😊	😖 😣 😐 🙂 😊

Date

....

Notes for Today

_____
_____
_____
_____
_____
_____
_____
_____
_____

Feeding

_____
_____

Changing

_____
_____

Sleep/Naps

_____
_____

Parent's Day: ☐ Extra crazy!   ☐ Survival Mode   ☐ OK
              ☐ Good   ☐ Super easy!

Baby's Mood	Your Mood
☹ 😕 😐 🙂 😊	☹ 😕 😐 🙂 😊

Date

....

Notes for Today

_____
_____
_____
_____
_____
_____
_____
_____
_____

Feeding

_____
_____

Changing

_____
_____

Sleep/Naps

_____
_____

Parent's Day: ☐ Extra crazy! ☐ Survival Mode ☐ OK

☐ Good ☐ Super easy!

Baby's Mood	Your Mood
😣 😖 😐 🙂 😊	😣 😖 😐 🙂 😊

Date

....

Notes for Today

_____
_____
_____
_____
_____
_____
_____
_____
_____

Feeding

_____
_____
_____

Changing

_____
_____
_____

Sleep/Naps

_____
_____
_____

Parent's Day: ☐ Extra crazy! ☐ Survival Mode ☐ OK
☐ Good ☐ Super easy!

Baby's Mood	Your Mood
😖 😩 😐 🙂 😊	😖 😩 😐 🙂 😊

Date

....

Notes for Today

_____
_____
_____
_____
_____
_____
_____
_____
_____
_____

Feeding

_____
_____
_____

Changing

_____
_____
_____

Sleep/Naps

_____
_____
_____

Parent's Day: ☐ Extra crazy! ☐ Survival Mode ☐ OK

☐ Good ☐ Super easy!

Baby's Mood : Your Mood

Date

....

Notes for Today

_____
_____
_____
_____
_____
_____
_____
_____
_____
_____

Feeding

_____
_____
_____

Changing

_____
_____
_____

Sleep/Naps

_____
_____
_____

Parent's Day: ☐ Extra crazy! ☐ Survival Mode ☐ OK
               ☐ Good   ☐ Super easy!

Baby's Mood   Your Mood
☹ 😕 😐 🙂 ☺   ☹ 😕 😐 🙂 ☺

Date

....

Notes for Today

_____
_____
_____
_____
_____
_____
_____
_____
_____
_____

Feeding

_____
_____

Changing

_____
_____
_____

Sleep/Naps

_____
_____
_____

Parent's Day: ☐ Extra crazy! ☐ Survival Mode ☐ OK

☐ Good ☐ Super easy!

Baby's Mood	Your Mood
☹ 😐 😐 🙂 😊	☹ 😐 😐 🙂 😊

Date

....

Notes for Today

_____
_____
_____
_____
_____
_____
_____
_____
_____

Feeding

_____
_____
_____

Changing

_____
_____
_____

Sleep/Naps

_____
_____
_____

Parent's Day: ☐ Extra crazy! ☐ Survival Mode ☐ OK
☐ Good ☐ Super easy!

Baby's Mood : Your Mood
☹ ☺ ☺ ☺ ☺ : ☹ ☺ ☺ ☺ ☺

Date

··

Notes for Today

_____
_____
_____
_____
_____
_____
_____
_____
_____
_____

Feeding

_____
_____

Changing

_____
_____

Sleep/Naps

_____
_____

Parent's Day: ☐ Extra crazy! ☐ Survival Mode ☐ OK
☐ Good ☐ Super easy!

Baby's Mood ☹ ☹ ☺ ☺ ☺   Your Mood ☹ ☹ ☺ ☺ ☺

Date

....

Notes for Today

_____
_____
_____
_____
_____
_____
_____
_____
_____
_____

Feeding

_____
_____

Changing

_____
_____

Sleep/Naps

_____
_____

Parent's Day: ☐ Extra crazy! ☐ Survival Mode ☐ OK
☐ Good ☐ Super easy!

Baby's Mood	Your Mood
☹ 😐 😐 🙂 😊	☹ 😐 😐 🙂 😊

Date

....

Notes for Today

_____
_____
_____
_____
_____
_____
_____
_____
_____
_____

Feeding

_____
_____
_____

Changing

_____
_____
_____

Sleep/Naps

_____
_____
_____

Parent's Day: ☐ Extra crazy! ☐ Survival Mode ☐ OK

☐ Good ☐ Super easy!

Baby's Mood	Your Mood
☹ 😐 😐 🙂 😊	☹ 😐 😐 🙂 😊

Date

....

Notes for Today

_____
_____
_____
_____
_____
_____
_____
_____
_____
_____

Feeding

_____
_____
_____

Changing

_____
_____
_____

Sleep/Naps

_____
_____
_____

Parent's Day: ☐ Extra crazy! ☐ Survival Mode ☐ OK

☐ Good ☐ Super easy!

Baby's Mood	Your Mood
😣 😕 😐 🙂 😊	😣 😕 😐 🙂 😊

Date

....

Notes for Today

_____
_____
_____
_____
_____
_____
_____
_____
_____

Feeding

_____
_____

Changing

_____
_____

Sleep/Naps

_____
_____

Parent's Day: ☐ Extra crazy! ☐ Survival Mode ☐ OK

☐ Good ☐ Super easy!

Baby's Mood	Your Mood

Date

....

Notes for Today

_____
_____
_____
_____
_____
_____
_____
_____
_____

Feeding
_____
_____

Changing
_____
_____

Sleep/Naps
_____
_____

Parent's Day: ☐ Extra crazy! ☐ Survival Mode ☐ OK
☐ Good ☐ Super easy!

Baby's Mood	Your Mood
☹ 🙁 😐 🙂 😊	☹ 🙁 😐 🙂 😊

Date

....

Notes for Today

_____
_____
_____
_____
_____
_____
_____
_____
_____

Feeding

_____
_____
_____

Changing

_____
_____
_____

Sleep/Naps

_____
_____

Parent's Day: ☐ Extra crazy! ☐ Survival Mode ☐ OK

☐ Good ☐ Super easy!

Baby's Mood	Your Mood
☹ 😕 😐 🙂 😊	☹ 😕 😐 🙂 😊

Date

....

Notes for Today

_____
_____
_____
_____
_____
_____
_____
_____
_____

Feeding

_____
_____
_____

Changing

_____
_____
_____

Sleep/Naps

_____
_____
_____

Parent's Day: ☐ Extra crazy! ☐ Survival Mode ☐ OK

☐ Good ☐ Super easy!

Baby's Mood	Your Mood
☹ 😐 😐 🙂 😊	☹ 😐 😐 🙂 😊

Date

....

Notes for Today

_____
_____
_____
_____
_____
_____
_____
_____
_____

Feeding
_____
_____

Changing
_____
_____

Sleep/Naps
_____
_____

Parent's Day: ☐ Extra crazy! ☐ Survival Mode ☐ OK

☐ Good ☐ Super easy!

Baby's Mood	Your Mood

Date

....

Notes for Today

_____
_____
_____
_____
_____
_____
_____
_____
_____

Feeding

_____
_____

Changing

_____
_____

Sleep/Naps

_____
_____

Parent's Day: ☐ Extra crazy!   ☐ Survival Mode   ☐ OK
               ☐ Good   ☐ Super easy!

Baby's Mood	Your Mood
☹ 🙁 😐 🙂 😊	☹ 🙁 😐 🙂 😊

Date

....

Notes for Today

_____
_____
_____
_____
_____
_____
_____
_____
_____

Feeding

_____
_____
_____

Changing

_____
_____
_____

Sleep/Naps

_____
_____
_____

Parent's Day: ☐ Extra crazy!   ☐ Survival Mode   ☐ OK

☐ Good   ☐ Super easy!

Baby's Mood	Your Mood
☹ 😐 😐 🙂 😊	☹ 😐 😐 🙂 😊

Date

....

Notes for Today

_____
_____
_____
_____
_____
_____
_____
_____
_____

Feeding

_____
_____
_____

Changing

_____
_____
_____

Sleep/Naps

_____
_____
_____

Parent's Day: ☐ Extra crazy!   ☐ Survival Mode   ☐ OK

☐ Good   ☐ Super easy!

Baby's Mood	Your Mood
😣 😖 😐 🙂 😊	😣 😖 😐 🙂 😊

Date

....

Notes for Today

_____
_____
_____
_____
_____
_____
_____
_____
_____
_____

Feeding

_____
_____

Changing

_____
_____

Sleep/Naps

_____
_____

Parent's Day: ☐ Extra crazy! ☐ Survival Mode ☐ OK
☐ Good ☐ Super easy!

Baby's Mood	Your Mood
☹ ☹ 😐 🙂 😊	☹ ☹ 😐 🙂 😊

Date

....

Notes for Today

_____
_____
_____
_____
_____
_____
_____
_____
_____
_____

Feeding

_____
_____
_____

Changing

_____
_____
_____

Sleep/Naps

_____
_____
_____

Parent's Day: ☐ Extra crazy! ☐ Survival Mode ☐ OK

☐ Good ☐ Super easy!

Baby's Mood : Your Mood
☹ 🙁 😐 🙂 😊 : ☹ 🙁 😐 🙂 😊

Date

....

Notes for Today

_____
_____
_____
_____
_____
_____
_____
_____

Feeding

_____
_____
_____

Changing

_____
_____
_____

Sleep/Naps

_____
_____

Parent's Day: ☐ Extra crazy! ☐ Survival Mode ☐ OK

☐ Good ☐ Super easy!

Baby's Mood   Your Mood
☹ 😕 😐 🙂 😊   ☹ 😕 😐 🙂 😊

Date

....

Notes for Today

_____
_____
_____
_____
_____
_____
_____
_____
_____

Feeding

_____
_____
_____

Changing

_____
_____
_____

Sleep/Naps

_____
_____
_____

Parent's Day: ☐ Extra crazy! ☐ Survival Mode ☐ OK
☐ Good ☐ Super easy!

Baby's Mood	Your Mood
😣 😕 😐 🙂 😊	😣 😕 😐 🙂 😊

Date

....

Notes for Today

_____
_____
_____
_____
_____
_____
_____
_____
_____

Feeding

_____
_____

Changing

_____
_____

Sleep/Naps

_____
_____

Parent's Day: ☐ Extra crazy!   ☐ Survival Mode   ☐ OK
               ☐ Good   ☐ Super easy!

Baby's Mood	Your Mood
😣 😖 😐 🙂 😊	😣 😖 😐 🙂 😊

Date

....

Notes for Today

_____

_____

_____

_____

_____

_____

_____

_____

_____

Feeding

_____

_____

Changing

_____

_____

Sleep/Naps

_____

_____

Parent's Day: ☐ Extra crazy! ☐ Survival Mode ☐ OK

☐ Good ☐ Super easy!

Baby's Mood	Your Mood

Date

....

Notes for Today

_____
_____
_____
_____
_____
_____
_____
_____
_____
_____

Feeding

_____
_____
_____

Changing

_____
_____
_____

Sleep/Naps

_____
_____
_____

Parent's Day: ☐ Extra crazy! ☐ Survival Mode ☐ OK

☐ Good ☐ Super easy!

Baby's Mood	Your Mood
☹ 😐 😐 🙂 😊	☹ 😐 😐 🙂 😊

Date

....

Notes for Today

_____
_____
_____
_____
_____
_____
_____
_____
_____

Feeding

_____
_____
_____

Changing

_____
_____
_____

Sleep/Naps

_____
_____
_____

Parent's Day: ☐ Extra crazy! ☐ Survival Mode ☐ OK

☐ Good ☐ Super easy!

Baby's Mood	Your Mood
☹ 😐 😐 🙂 😊	☹ 😐 😐 🙂 😊

Date

....

Notes for Today

_____
_____
_____
_____
_____
_____
_____
_____
_____

Feeding

_____
_____

Changing

_____
_____

Sleep/Naps

_____
_____

Parent's Day: ☐ Extra crazy! ☐ Survival Mode ☐ OK

☐ Good ☐ Super easy!

Baby's Mood	Your Mood
😣 😖 😐 🙂 😊	😣 😖 😐 🙂 😊

Date

....

Notes for Today

_____
_____
_____
_____
_____
_____
_____
_____
_____

Feeding

_____
_____

Changing

_____
_____

Sleep/Naps

_____
_____

Parent's Day: ☐ Extra crazy! ☐ Survival Mode ☐ OK
              ☐ Good   ☐ Super easy!

Baby's Mood	Your Mood
☹ 😐 😐 🙂 😊	☹ 😐 😐 🙂 😊

Date

....

Notes for Today

_____
_____
_____
_____
_____
_____
_____
_____
_____

Feeding

_____
_____
_____

Changing

_____
_____
_____

Sleep/Naps

_____
_____
_____

Parent's Day: ☐ Extra crazy! ☐ Survival Mode ☐ OK

☐ Good ☐ Super easy!

Baby's Mood   Your Mood

☹ ☹ ☺ ☺ ☺   ☹ ☹ ☺ ☺ ☺

Date

....

Notes for Today

_____
_____
_____
_____
_____
_____
_____
_____
_____

Feeding

_____
_____
_____

Changing

_____
_____
_____

Sleep/Naps

_____
_____
_____

Parent's Day: ☐ Extra crazy! ☐ Survival Mode ☐ OK
☐ Good ☐ Super easy!

Baby's Mood	Your Mood
☹ 😕 😐 🙂 ☺	☹ 😕 😐 🙂 ☺

Date

....

Notes for Today

_____
_____
_____
_____
_____
_____
_____
_____
_____

Feeding

_____
_____

Changing

_____
_____

Sleep/Naps

_____
_____

Parent's Day: ☐ Extra crazy! ☐ Survival Mode ☐ OK

☐ Good ☐ Super easy!

Baby's Mood

Your Mood

Date

....

Notes for Today

_____
_____
_____
_____
_____
_____
_____
_____
_____

Feeding

_____
_____

Changing

_____
_____

Sleep/Naps

_____
_____

Parent's Day: ☐ Extra crazy! ☐ Survival Mode ☐ OK
☐ Good ☐ Super easy!

Baby's Mood   Your Mood
☹ 😕 😐 🙂 😊   ☹ 😕 😐 🙂 😊

Date

··

Notes for Today

_____
_____
_____
_____
_____
_____
_____
_____
_____

Feeding

_____
_____

Changing

_____
_____
_____

Sleep/Naps

_____
_____

Parent's Day: ☐ Extra crazy! ☐ Survival Mode ☐ OK

☐ Good ☐ Super easy!

Baby's Mood ☹ 😐 😐 🙂 😊 : Your Mood ☹ 😐 😐 🙂 😊

Date

....

Notes for Today

_____
_____
_____
_____
_____
_____
_____
_____
_____

Feeding

_____
_____
_____

Changing

_____
_____
_____

Sleep/Naps

_____
_____
_____

Parent's Day: ☐ Extra crazy!   ☐ Survival Mode   ☐ OK
              ☐ Good   ☐ Super easy!

Baby's Mood	Your Mood
☹ 😕 😐 🙂 ☺	☹ 😕 😐 🙂 ☺

Date

....

Notes for Today

_____
_____
_____
_____
_____
_____
_____
_____
_____
_____

Feeding

_____
_____
_____

Changing

_____
_____
_____

Sleep/Naps

_____
_____
_____

Parent's Day: ☐ Extra crazy! ☐ Survival Mode ☐ OK
☐ Good ☐ Super easy!

Baby's Mood   Your Mood
☹ 😕 😐 🙂 😊   ☹ 😕 😐 🙂 😊

Date

....

Notes for Today

_____
_____
_____
_____
_____
_____
_____
_____
_____

Feeding

_____
_____

Changing

_____
_____

Sleep/Naps

_____
_____

Parent's Day: ☐ Extra crazy! ☐ Survival Mode ☐ OK

☐ Good ☐ Super easy!

Baby's Mood	Your Mood
☹ 🙁 😐 🙂 😊	☹ 🙁 😐 🙂 😊

Date

....

Notes for Today

_____
_____
_____
_____
_____
_____
_____
_____
_____

Feeding

_____
_____
_____

Changing

_____
_____
_____

Sleep/Naps

_____
_____
_____

Parent's Day: ☐ Extra crazy! ☐ Survival Mode ☐ OK

☐ Good ☐ Super easy!

Baby's Mood	Your Mood
☹ ☹ ☺ ☺ ☺	☹ ☹ ☺ ☺ ☺

Date

....

Notes for Today

_____
_____
_____
_____
_____
_____
_____
_____
_____
_____
_____
_____

Feeding

_____
_____
_____

Changing

_____
_____
_____

Sleep/Naps

_____
_____
_____

Parent's Day: ☐ Extra crazy! ☐ Survival Mode ☐ OK

☐ Good ☐ Super easy!

Baby's Mood	Your Mood
😣 😕 😐 🙂 😊	😣 😕 😐 🙂 😊

Date

....

Notes for Today

_____
_____
_____
_____
_____
_____
_____
_____
_____
_____

Feeding

_____
_____
_____

Changing

_____
_____
_____

Sleep/Naps

_____
_____
_____

Parent's Day: ☐ Extra crazy!   ☐ Survival Mode   ☐ OK

☐ Good   ☐ Super easy!

Baby's Mood	Your Mood
😣 😖 😐 🙂 😊	😣 😖 😐 🙂 😊

Date

....

Notes for Today

_____
_____
_____
_____
_____
_____
_____
_____
_____
_____

Feeding

_____
_____

Changing

_____
_____

Sleep/Naps

_____
_____

Parent's Day: ☐ Extra crazy! ☐ Survival Mode ☐ OK

☐ Good ☐ Super easy!

Baby's Mood	Your Mood
☹ 😐 😐 🙂 😊	☹ 😐 😐 🙂 😊

Date

....

Notes for Today

_____
_____
_____
_____
_____
_____
_____
_____
_____

Feeding

_____
_____
_____

Changing

_____
_____
_____

Sleep/Naps

_____
_____
_____

Parent's Day: ☐ Extra crazy! ☐ Survival Mode ☐ OK

☐ Good ☐ Super easy!

Baby's Mood	Your Mood
☹ 😐 😐 😊 😊	☹ 😐 😐 😊 😊

Date

....

Notes for Today

_____
_____
_____
_____
_____
_____
_____
_____
_____

Feeding

_____
_____
_____

Changing

_____
_____
_____

Sleep/Naps

_____
_____
_____

Parent's Day: ☐ Extra crazy! ☐ Survival Mode ☐ OK
☐ Good ☐ Super easy!

Baby's Mood	Your Mood
☹ 😐 😐 🙂 😊	☹ 😐 😐 🙂 😊

Date

....

Notes for Today

_____
_____
_____
_____
_____
_____
_____
_____
_____

Feeding

_____
_____

Changing

_____
_____

Sleep/Naps

_____
_____

Parent's Day: ☐ Extra crazy! ☐ Survival Mode ☐ OK

☐ Good ☐ Super easy!

Baby's Mood
☹ ☹ ☺ ☺ ☺

Your Mood
☹ ☹ ☺ ☺ ☺

Date

....

Notes for Today

_____
_____
_____
_____
_____
_____
_____
_____
_____

Feeding

_____
_____
_____

Changing

_____
_____

Sleep/Naps

_____
_____

Parent's Day: ☐ Extra crazy! ☐ Survival Mode ☐ OK

☐ Good ☐ Super easy!

Baby's Mood	Your Mood
☹ 😐 😐 🙂 ☺	☹ 😐 😐 🙂 ☺

Date

....

Notes for Today

_____
_____
_____
_____
_____
_____
_____
_____
_____

Feeding

_____
_____

Changing

_____
_____

Sleep/Naps

_____
_____

Parent's Day: ☐ Extra crazy! ☐ Survival Mode ☐ OK

☐ Good ☐ Super easy!

Baby's Mood	Your Mood
☹ 😐 😐 🙂 😊	☹ 😐 😐 🙂 😊

Date

....

Notes for Today

_____
_____
_____
_____
_____
_____
_____
_____
_____

Feeding

_____
_____
_____

Changing

_____
_____
_____

Sleep/Naps

_____
_____
_____

Parent's Day: ☐ Extra crazy! ☐ Survival Mode ☐ OK
☐ Good ☐ Super easy!

Baby's Mood   Your Mood
☹ 😐 😐 🙂 ☺   ☹ 😐 😐 🙂 ☺

Date

....

Notes for Today

_____
_____
_____
_____
_____
_____
_____
_____
_____

Feeding

_____
_____

Changing

_____
_____

Sleep/Naps

_____
_____

Parent's Day: ☐ Extra crazy! ☐ Survival Mode ☐ OK

☐ Good ☐ Super easy!

Baby's Mood	Your Mood
☹ 😕 😐 🙂 😊	☹ 😕 😐 🙂 😊

Date

....

Notes for Today

_____
_____
_____
_____
_____
_____
_____
_____
_____

Feeding

_____
_____
_____

Changing

_____
_____
_____

Sleep/Naps

_____
_____
_____

Parent's Day: ☐ Extra crazy! ☐ Survival Mode ☐ OK

☐ Good ☐ Super easy!

Baby's Mood	Your Mood
☹ ☹ ☺ ☺ ☺	☹ ☹ ☺ ☺ ☺

Date

....

Notes for Today

_____
_____
_____
_____
_____
_____
_____
_____
_____

Feeding

_____
_____

Changing

_____
_____

Sleep/Naps

_____
_____

Parent's Day: ☐ Extra crazy! ☐ Survival Mode ☐ OK

☐ Good ☐ Super easy!

Baby's Mood	Your Mood
☹ 😐 😐 🙂 ☺	☹ 😐 😐 🙂 ☺

Date

....

Notes for Today

_____
_____
_____
_____
_____
_____
_____
_____
_____
_____
_____

Feeding

_____
_____
_____

Changing

_____
_____
_____

Sleep/Naps

_____
_____
_____

Parent's Day: ☐ Extra crazy! ☐ Survival Mode ☐ OK
☐ Good ☐ Super easy!

Baby's Mood	Your Mood
😣 😕 😐 🙂 😊	😣 😕 😐 🙂 😊

Date

....

Notes for Today

_____
_____
_____
_____
_____
_____
_____
_____
_____
_____

Feeding

_____
_____

Changing

_____
_____

Sleep/Naps

_____
_____

Parent's Day: ☐ Extra crazy! ☐ Survival Mode ☐ OK
☐ Good ☐ Super easy!

Baby's Mood	Your Mood
😣 😖 😐 🙂 😊	😣 😖 😐 🙂 😊

Date

··

Notes for Today

_____
_____
_____
_____
_____
_____
_____
_____
_____
_____

Feeding

_____
_____

Changing

_____
_____

Sleep/Naps

_____
_____

Parent's Day: ☐ Extra crazy! ☐ Survival Mode ☐ OK

☐ Good ☐ Super easy!

Baby's Mood : Your Mood

☹ 😐 😐 🙂 😊 : ☹ 😐 😐 🙂 😊

Date

....

Notes for Today

Feeding

Changing

Sleep/Naps

Parent's Day: ☐ Extra crazy! ☐ Survival Mode ☐ OK

☐ Good ☐ Super easy!

Baby's Mood	Your Mood
☹ ☺ ☺ ☺ ☺	☹ ☺ ☺ ☺ ☺

Date

....

Notes for Today

_____
_____
_____
_____
_____
_____
_____
_____
_____
_____

Feeding

_____
_____

Changing

_____
_____

Sleep/Naps

_____
_____

Parent's Day: ☐ Extra crazy! ☐ Survival Mode ☐ OK
☐ Good ☐ Super easy!

Baby's Mood   Your Mood
😣 😖 😐 🙂 😊 : 😣 😖 😐 🙂 😊

Date

....

Notes for Today

_____
_____
_____
_____
_____
_____
_____
_____
_____

Feeding

_____
_____

Changing

_____
_____

Sleep/Naps

_____
_____

Parent's Day: ☐ Extra crazy! ☐ Survival Mode ☐ OK

☐ Good ☐ Super easy!

Baby's Mood	Your Mood
☹ 😖 😐 🙂 ☺	☹ 😖 😐 🙂 ☺

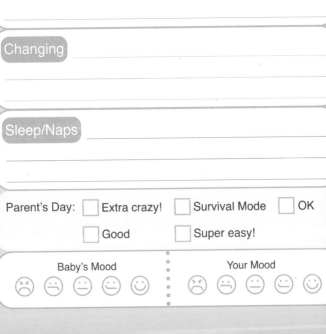

Date

....

Notes for Today

_____
_____
_____
_____
_____
_____
_____
_____
_____

Feeding

_____
_____
_____

Changing

_____
_____
_____

Sleep/Naps

_____
_____
_____

Parent's Day: ☐ Extra crazy! ☐ Survival Mode ☐ OK
☐ Good ☐ Super easy!

Baby's Mood ☹ 😕 😐 🙂 😊 : Your Mood ☹ 😕 😐 🙂 😊

Date

....

Notes for Today

_____
_____
_____
_____
_____
_____
_____
_____
_____
_____

Feeding

_____
_____
_____

Changing

_____
_____
_____

Sleep/Naps

_____
_____
_____

Parent's Day: ☐ Extra crazy! ☐ Survival Mode ☐ OK

☐ Good ☐ Super easy!

Baby's Mood	Your Mood

Date

....

Notes for Today

_____
_____
_____
_____
_____
_____
_____
_____
_____

Feeding

_____
_____

Changing

_____
_____

Sleep/Naps

_____
_____

Parent's Day: ☐ Extra crazy! ☐ Survival Mode ☐ OK
☐ Good ☐ Super easy!

Baby's Mood
☹ 🙁 😐 🙂 😊

Your Mood
☹ 🙁 😐 🙂 😊

Date

....

Notes for Today

_____
_____
_____
_____
_____
_____
_____
_____
_____

Feeding

_____
_____

Changing

_____
_____

Sleep/Naps

_____
_____

Parent's Day: ☐ Extra crazy! ☐ Survival Mode ☐ OK

☐ Good ☐ Super easy!

Baby's Mood   Your Mood

Date

....

Notes for Today

_____
_____
_____
_____
_____
_____
_____
_____
_____

Feeding

_____
_____

Changing

_____
_____

Sleep/Naps

_____
_____

Parent's Day: ☐ Extra crazy! ☐ Survival Mode ☐ OK

☐ Good ☐ Super easy!

Baby's Mood	Your Mood
☹ 😐 😐 🙂 ☺	☹ 😐 😐 🙂 ☺

Date

Notes for Today

_____
_____
_____
_____
_____
_____
_____
_____

Feeding
_____
_____

Changing
_____
_____

Sleep/Naps
_____
_____

Parent's Day: ☐ Extra crazy! ☐ Survival Mode ☐ OK
☐ Good ☐ Super easy!

Baby's Mood   Your Mood
☹ 😕 😐 🙂 😊   ☹ 😕 😐 🙂 😊

Date

....

Notes for Today

_____
_____
_____
_____
_____
_____
_____
_____

Feeding

_____
_____
_____

Changing

_____
_____
_____

Sleep/Naps

_____
_____
_____

Parent's Day: ☐ Extra crazy! ☐ Survival Mode ☐ OK
              ☐ Good   ☐ Super easy!

Baby's Mood   Your Mood
😣 😕 😐 🙂 😊   😣 😕 😐 🙂 😊

Date

....

Notes for Today

_____
_____
_____
_____
_____
_____
_____
_____
_____

Feeding
_____
_____
_____

Changing
_____
_____

Sleep/Naps
_____
_____
_____

Parent's Day: ☐ Extra crazy! ☐ Survival Mode ☐ OK

☐ Good ☐ Super easy!

Baby's Mood	Your Mood
😣 😑 😐 🙂 😊	😣 😑 😐 🙂 😊

Date

....

Notes for Today

_____
_____
_____
_____
_____
_____
_____
_____
_____

Feeding

_____
_____
_____

Changing

_____
_____
_____

Sleep/Naps

_____
_____
_____

Parent's Day: ☐ Extra crazy! ☐ Survival Mode ☐ OK
☐ Good ☐ Super easy!

Baby's Mood	Your Mood
☹ 😕 😐 🙂 😊	☹ 😕 😐 🙂 😊

Date

....

Notes for Today

_____
_____
_____
_____
_____
_____
_____
_____

Feeding

_____
_____
_____

Changing

_____
_____
_____

Sleep/Naps

_____
_____
_____

Parent's Day: ☐ Extra crazy! ☐ Survival Mode ☐ OK

☐ Good ☐ Super easy!

Baby's Mood	Your Mood
☹ 😕 😐 🙂 😊	☹ 😕 😐 🙂 😊

Date

Notes for Today

Feeding

Changing

Sleep/Naps

Parent's Day: ☐ Extra crazy! ☐ Survival Mode ☐ OK

☐ Good ☐ Super easy!

Baby's Mood
☹ 😕 😐 🙂 😊

Your Mood
☹ 😕 😐 🙂 😊

Date

....

Notes for Today

_____
_____
_____
_____
_____
_____
_____
_____
_____
_____

Feeding

_____
_____
_____

Changing

_____
_____
_____

Sleep/Naps

_____
_____
_____

Parent's Day: ☐ Extra crazy! ☐ Survival Mode ☐ OK

☐ Good ☐ Super easy!

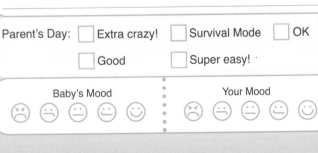

Baby's Mood ☹ 😕 😐 🙂 😊   Your Mood ☹ 😕 😐 🙂 😊

Date

....

Notes for Today

_____
_____
_____
_____
_____
_____
_____
_____
_____
_____

Feeding

_____
_____

Changing

_____
_____

Sleep/Naps

_____
_____

Parent's Day: ☐ Extra crazy! ☐ Survival Mode ☐ OK
☐ Good ☐ Super easy!

Baby's Mood
☹ 😕 😐 🙂 ☺

Your Mood
☹ 😕 😐 🙂 ☺

Date

....

Notes for Today

_____
_____
_____
_____
_____
_____
_____
_____
_____
_____

Feeding

_____
_____
_____

Changing

_____
_____
_____

Sleep/Naps

_____
_____
_____

Parent's Day: ☐ Extra crazy!   ☐ Survival Mode   ☐ OK

☐ Good   ☐ Super easy!

Baby's Mood	Your Mood
☹ 😐 😐 🙂 😊	☹ 😐 😐 🙂 😊

Date

....

Notes for Today

_____
_____
_____
_____
_____
_____
_____
_____
_____
_____

Feeding

_____
_____
_____

Changing

_____
_____
_____

Sleep/Naps

_____
_____
_____

Parent's Day: ☐ Extra crazy! ☐ Survival Mode ☐ OK

☐ Good ☐ Super easy!

Baby's Mood	Your Mood
☹ 😐 😐 🙂 😊	☹ 😐 😐 🙂 😊

Date

....

Notes for Today

_____
_____
_____
_____
_____
_____
_____
_____
_____

Feeding

_____
_____

Changing

_____
_____

Sleep/Naps

_____
_____

Parent's Day: ☐ Extra crazy! ☐ Survival Mode ☐ OK
☐ Good ☐ Super easy!

Baby's Mood	Your Mood

Date

....

Notes for Today

_____
_____
_____
_____
_____
_____
_____
_____
_____

Feeding

_____
_____

Changing

_____
_____

Sleep/Naps

_____
_____

Parent's Day: ☐ Extra crazy! ☐ Survival Mode ☐ OK
☐ Good ☐ Super easy!

Baby's Mood	Your Mood
☹ ☺ ☺ ☺ ☺	☹ ☺ ☺ ☺ ☺

Date

....

Notes for Today

_____
_____
_____
_____
_____
_____
_____
_____
_____

Feeding

_____
_____
_____

Changing

_____
_____
_____

Sleep/Naps

_____
_____
_____

Parent's Day: ☐ Extra crazy!   ☐ Survival Mode   ☐ OK
              ☐ Good   ☐ Super easy!

Baby's Mood	Your Mood
😣 😖 😐 🙂 😊	😣 😖 😐 🙂 😊

Date

....

Notes for Today

_____
_____
_____
_____
_____
_____
_____
_____
_____

Feeding

_____
_____
_____

Changing

_____
_____
_____

Sleep/Naps

_____
_____
_____

Parent's Day: ☐ Extra crazy! ☐ Survival Mode ☐ OK

☐ Good ☐ Super easy!

Baby's Mood	Your Mood
☹ 😐 😐 🙂 ☺	☹ 😐 😐 🙂 ☺

Date

....

Notes for Today

_____
_____
_____
_____
_____
_____
_____
_____
_____
_____

Feeding

_____
_____

Changing

_____
_____

Sleep/Naps

_____
_____

Parent's Day: ☐ Extra crazy! ☐ Survival Mode ☐ OK

☐ Good ☐ Super easy!

Baby's Mood	Your Mood

Date

....

Notes for Today

_____
_____
_____
_____
_____
_____
_____
_____
_____

Feeding

_____
_____

Changing

_____
_____

Sleep/Naps

_____
_____

Parent's Day: ☐ Extra crazy! ☐ Survival Mode ☐ OK

☐ Good ☐ Super easy!

Baby's Mood	Your Mood
☹ 😕 😐 🙂 😊	☹ 😕 😐 🙂 😊

Date

....

Notes for Today

_____
_____
_____
_____
_____
_____
_____
_____
_____

Feeding

_____
_____
_____

Changing

_____
_____
_____

Sleep/Naps

_____
_____

Parent's Day: ☐ Extra crazy! ☐ Survival Mode ☐ OK

☐ Good ☐ Super easy!

Baby's Mood   Your Mood

☹ 😕 😐 🙂 😊   ☹ 😕 😐 🙂 😊

Date

....

Notes for Today

_____
_____
_____
_____
_____
_____
_____
_____
_____

Feeding

_____
_____

Changing

_____
_____

Sleep/Naps

_____
_____

Parent's Day: ☐ Extra crazy! ☐ Survival Mode ☐ OK
☐ Good ☐ Super easy!

Baby's Mood	Your Mood
☹ 😐 😐 🙂 😊	☹ 😐 😐 🙂 😊

Date

....

Notes for Today

_____

_____

_____

_____

_____

_____

_____

_____

_____

Feeding

_____

_____

Changing

_____

_____

Sleep/Naps

_____

_____

Parent's Day: ☐ Extra crazy! ☐ Survival Mode ☐ OK

☐ Good ☐ Super easy!

Baby's Mood	Your Mood
😣 😖 😐 🙂 😊	😣 😖 😐 🙂 😊

Date

....

Notes for Today

_____
_____
_____
_____
_____
_____
_____
_____
_____

Feeding

_____
_____

Changing

_____
_____

Sleep/Naps

_____
_____

Parent's Day: ☐ Extra crazy!   ☐ Survival Mode   ☐ OK

☐ Good   ☐ Super easy!

Baby's Mood	Your Mood
☹ 😐 😐 🙂 😊	☹ 😐 😐 🙂 😊

Date

....

Notes for Today

_____
_____
_____
_____
_____
_____
_____
_____
_____

Feeding

_____
_____
_____

Changing

_____
_____
_____

Sleep/Naps

_____
_____

Parent's Day: ☐ Extra crazy! ☐ Survival Mode ☐ OK

☐ Good ☐ Super easy!

Baby's Mood	Your Mood
☹ 😐 😐 🙂 😊	☹ 😐 😐 🙂 😊

Date

....

Notes for Today

_____
_____
_____
_____
_____
_____
_____
_____
_____

Feeding

_____
_____
_____

Changing

_____
_____
_____

Sleep/Naps

_____
_____
_____

Parent's Day: ☐ Extra crazy! ☐ Survival Mode ☐ OK

☐ Good ☐ Super easy!

Baby's Mood	Your Mood
☹ 😐 😐 🙂 😊	☹ 😐 😐 🙂 😊

Date

....

Notes for Today

_____
_____
_____
_____
_____
_____
_____
_____
_____
_____

Feeding

_____
_____

Changing

_____
_____

Sleep/Naps

_____
_____

Parent's Day: ☐ Extra crazy! ☐ Survival Mode ☐ OK
☐ Good ☐ Super easy!

Baby's Mood   Your Mood
☹ 🙁 😐 🙂 😊   ☹ 🙁 😐 🙂 😊

Date

....

Notes for Today

_____
_____
_____
_____
_____
_____
_____
_____
_____
_____

Feeding

_____
_____
_____

Changing

_____
_____
_____

Sleep/Naps

_____
_____
_____

Parent's Day: ☐ Extra crazy! ☐ Survival Mode ☐ OK

☐ Good ☐ Super easy!

Baby's Mood   Your Mood

☹ 🙁 😐 🙂 😊   ☹ 🙁 😐 🙂 😊

Date

....

Notes for Today

_____
_____
_____
_____
_____
_____
_____
_____
_____

Feeding

_____
_____
_____

Changing

_____
_____
_____

Sleep/Naps

_____
_____
_____

Parent's Day: ☐ Extra crazy! ☐ Survival Mode ☐ OK

☐ Good ☐ Super easy!

Baby's Mood	Your Mood
😣 😔 😐 🙂 😊	😣 😔 😐 🙂 😊

Date

....

Notes for Today

_____
_____
_____
_____
_____
_____
_____
_____
_____
_____

Feeding

_____
_____
_____

Changing

_____
_____
_____

Sleep/Naps

_____
_____
_____

Parent's Day: ☐ Extra crazy!   ☐ Survival Mode   ☐ OK
☐ Good   ☐ Super easy!

Baby's Mood	Your Mood
☹ 😐 😐 🙂 ☺	☹ 😐 😐 🙂 ☺

Date

....

Notes for Today

_____
_____
_____
_____
_____
_____
_____
_____
_____

Feeding

_____
_____

Changing

_____
_____

Sleep/Naps

_____
_____

Parent's Day: ☐ Extra crazy! ☐ Survival Mode ☐ OK

☐ Good ☐ Super easy!

Baby's Mood	Your Mood
😖 😩 😐 🙂 😊	😖 😩 😐 🙂 😊

Date

....

Notes for Today

_____
_____
_____
_____
_____
_____
_____
_____
_____

Feeding

_____
_____

Changing

_____
_____

Sleep/Naps

_____
_____

Parent's Day: ☐ Extra crazy! ☐ Survival Mode ☐ OK ☐ Good ☐ Super easy!

Baby's Mood	Your Mood
☹ 😕 😐 🙂 ☺	☹ 😕 😐 🙂 ☺

Date

······································

Notes for Today

_____
_____
_____
_____
_____
_____
_____
_____
_____

Feeding

_____
_____
_____

Changing

_____
_____
_____

Sleep/Naps

_____
_____
_____

Parent's Day: ☐ Extra crazy! ☐ Survival Mode ☐ OK
☐ Good ☐ Super easy!

Baby's Mood	Your Mood

Date

....

Notes for Today

_____
_____
_____
_____
_____
_____
_____
_____
_____
_____

Feeding

_____
_____
_____

Changing

_____
_____
_____

Sleep/Naps

_____
_____
_____

Parent's Day: ☐ Extra crazy! ☐ Survival Mode ☐ OK
☐ Good ☐ Super easy!

Baby's Mood	Your Mood
☹ ☹ ☹ ☺ ☺	☹ ☹ ☹ ☺ ☺

Date

....

Notes for Today

_____
_____
_____
_____
_____
_____
_____
_____
_____
_____

Feeding

_____
_____
_____

Changing

_____
_____
_____

Sleep/Naps

_____
_____
_____

Parent's Day: ☐ Extra crazy! ☐ Survival Mode ☐ OK

☐ Good ☐ Super easy!

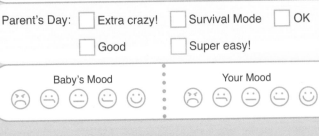

Baby's Mood   Your Mood

Date

....

Notes for Today

_____
_____
_____
_____
_____
_____
_____
_____
_____

Feeding

_____
_____

Changing

_____
_____

Sleep/Naps

_____
_____

Parent's Day: ☐ Extra crazy! ☐ Survival Mode ☐ OK
               ☐ Good   ☐ Super easy!

Baby's Mood	Your Mood
☹ 😐 😐 🙂 😊	☹ 😐 😐 🙂 😊

Date

....

Notes for Today

_____
_____
_____
_____
_____
_____
_____
_____
_____

Feeding

_____
_____
_____

Changing

_____
_____
_____

Sleep/Naps

_____
_____
_____

Parent's Day: ☐ Extra crazy! ☐ Survival Mode ☐ OK

☐ Good ☐ Super easy!

Baby's Mood	Your Mood
😖 😕 😐 🙂 😊	😖 😕 😐 🙂 😊

Date

....

Notes for Today

_____
_____
_____
_____
_____
_____
_____
_____
_____

Feeding
_____
_____

Changing
_____
_____
_____

Sleep/Naps
_____
_____

Parent's Day: ☐ Extra crazy! ☐ Survival Mode ☐ OK

☐ Good ☐ Super easy!

Baby's Mood	Your Mood
☹ ☺ ☺ ☺ ☺	☹ ☺ ☺ ☺ ☺

Date

....

Notes for Today

_____
_____
_____
_____
_____
_____
_____
_____
_____

Feeding

_____
_____

Changing

_____
_____

Sleep/Naps

_____
_____

Parent's Day: ☐ Extra crazy! ☐ Survival Mode ☐ OK

☐ Good ☐ Super easy!

Baby's Mood	Your Mood
☹ 😦 😐 🙂 😊	☹ 😦 😐 🙂 😊

Date

....

Notes for Today

_____
_____
_____
_____
_____
_____
_____
_____
_____

Feeding

_____
_____
_____

Changing

_____
_____
_____

Sleep/Naps

_____
_____
_____

Parent's Day: ☐ Extra crazy! ☐ Survival Mode ☐ OK
☐ Good ☐ Super easy!

Baby's Mood	Your Mood
☹ 😐 😐 🙂 😊	☹ 😐 😐 🙂 😊

Date

....

Notes for Today

_____
_____
_____
_____
_____
_____
_____
_____

Feeding

_____
_____

Changing

_____
_____

Sleep/Naps

_____
_____

Parent's Day: ☐ Extra crazy! ☐ Survival Mode ☐ OK

☐ Good ☐ Super easy!

Baby's Mood	Your Mood
😫 😕 😐 🙂 😊	😫 😕 😐 🙂 😊

Date

....

Notes for Today

_____
_____
_____
_____
_____
_____
_____
_____
_____

Feeding

_____
_____

Changing

_____
_____

Sleep/Naps

_____
_____

Parent's Day: ☐ Extra crazy! ☐ Survival Mode ☐ OK
☐ Good ☐ Super easy!

Baby's Mood	Your Mood
😣 😐 😑 🙂 😊	😣 😐 😑 🙂 😊

Date

....

Notes for Today

_____
_____
_____
_____
_____
_____
_____
_____
_____

Feeding

_____
_____

Changing

_____
_____

Sleep/Naps

_____
_____

Parent's Day: ☐ Extra crazy! ☐ Survival Mode ☐ OK

☐ Good ☐ Super easy!

Baby's Mood   Your Mood

☹ 😕 😐 🙂 😊   ☹ 😕 😐 🙂 😊

Date

....

Notes for Today

_____
_____
_____
_____
_____
_____
_____
_____
_____

Feeding

_____
_____

Changing

_____
_____

Sleep/Naps

_____
_____

Parent's Day: ☐ Extra crazy!   ☐ Survival Mode   ☐ OK

☐ Good   ☐ Super easy!

Baby's Mood	Your Mood
☹ 😐 😐 🙂 😊	☹ 😐 😐 🙂 😊

Date

....

Notes for Today

_____
_____
_____
_____
_____
_____
_____
_____
_____

Feeding

_____
_____

Changing

_____
_____

Sleep/Naps

_____
_____

Parent's Day: ☐ Extra crazy! ☐ Survival Mode ☐ OK

☐ Good ☐ Super easy!

Baby's Mood	Your Mood
☹ ☹ ☺ ☺ ☺	☹ ☹ ☺ ☺ ☺

Date

....

Notes for Today

_____
_____
_____
_____
_____
_____
_____
_____
_____
_____

Feeding

_____
_____
_____

Changing

_____
_____
_____

Sleep/Naps

_____
_____
_____

Parent's Day: ☐ Extra crazy! ☐ Survival Mode ☐ OK
☐ Good ☐ Super easy!

Baby's Mood	Your Mood
☹ 😕 😐 🙂 😊	☹ 😕 😐 🙂 😊

Date

....

Notes for Today

_____

_____

_____

_____

_____

_____

_____

_____

_____

Feeding

_____

_____

Changing

_____

_____

Sleep/Naps

_____

_____

Parent's Day: ☐ Extra crazy! ☐ Survival Mode ☐ OK

☐ Good ☐ Super easy!

Baby's Mood	Your Mood

Date

....

Notes for Today

_____
_____
_____
_____
_____
_____
_____
_____
_____
_____

Feeding

_____
_____
_____

Changing

_____
_____
_____

Sleep/Naps

_____
_____
_____

Parent's Day: ☐ Extra crazy! ☐ Survival Mode ☐ OK

☐ Good ☐ Super easy!

Baby's Mood	Your Mood
☹ 😕 😐 🙂 😊	☹ 😕 😐 🙂 😊

Date

....

Notes for Today

_____
_____
_____
_____
_____
_____
_____
_____
_____

Feeding

_____
_____
_____

Changing

_____
_____
_____

Sleep/Naps

_____
_____
_____

Parent's Day: ☐ Extra crazy! ☐ Survival Mode ☐ OK

☐ Good ☐ Super easy!

Baby's Mood	Your Mood
☹ 😐 😐 😐 ☺	☹ 😐 😐 😐 ☺

Date

....

Notes for Today

_____
_____
_____
_____
_____
_____
_____
_____
_____
_____

Feeding

_____
_____
_____

Changing

_____
_____
_____

Sleep/Naps

_____
_____
_____

Parent's Day: ☐ Extra crazy! ☐ Survival Mode ☐ OK

☐ Good ☐ Super easy!

Baby's Mood	Your Mood
☹ 😐 😐 🙂 😊	☹ 😐 😐 🙂 😊

Date

....

Notes for Today

_____
_____
_____
_____
_____
_____
_____
_____
_____

Feeding

_____
_____

Changing

_____
_____

Sleep/Naps

_____
_____

Parent's Day: ☐ Extra crazy! ☐ Survival Mode ☐ OK

☐ Good ☐ Super easy!

Baby's Mood	Your Mood

Date

....

Notes for Today

_____
_____
_____
_____
_____
_____
_____
_____
_____

Feeding

_____
_____

Changing

_____
_____

Sleep/Naps

_____
_____

Parent's Day: ☐ Extra crazy! ☐ Survival Mode ☐ OK
☐ Good ☐ Super easy!

Baby's Mood   Your Mood
☹ ☺ ☺ ☺ ☺   ☹ ☺ ☺ ☺ ☺

Date

....

Notes for Today

_____
_____
_____
_____
_____
_____
_____
_____
_____

Feeding

_____
_____

Changing

_____
_____

Sleep/Naps

_____
_____

Parent's Day: ☐ Extra crazy! ☐ Survival Mode ☐ OK

☐ Good ☐ Super easy!

Baby's Mood	Your Mood
☹ 😐 😐 🙂 😊	☹ 😐 😐 🙂 😊

Date

....

Notes for Today

_____
_____
_____
_____
_____
_____
_____
_____
_____
_____

Feeding

_____
_____
_____

Changing

_____
_____
_____

Sleep/Naps

_____
_____
_____

Parent's Day: ☐ Extra crazy! ☐ Survival Mode ☐ OK

☐ Good ☐ Super easy!

Baby's Mood	Your Mood
☹ 😐 😐 🙂 😊	☹ 😐 😐 🙂 😊

Date

....

Notes for Today

_____
_____
_____
_____
_____
_____
_____
_____
_____

Feeding

_____
_____

Changing

_____
_____

Sleep/Naps

_____
_____

Parent's Day: ☐ Extra crazy! ☐ Survival Mode ☐ OK
☐ Good ☐ Super easy!

Baby's Mood	Your Mood
😣 😒 😐 🙂 😊	😣 😒 😐 🙂 😊

Date

....

Notes for Today

_____
_____
_____
_____
_____
_____
_____
_____
_____
_____

Feeding

_____
_____

Changing

_____
_____

Sleep/Naps

_____
_____

Parent's Day: ☐ Extra crazy! ☐ Survival Mode ☐ OK
☐ Good ☐ Super easy!

Baby's Mood	Your Mood
☹ 😐 😐 🙂 😊	☹ 😐 😐 🙂 😊

Date

··

Notes for Today

_____
_____
_____
_____
_____
_____
_____
_____
_____

Feeding

_____
_____
_____

Changing

_____
_____
_____

Sleep/Naps

_____
_____

Parent's Day: ☐ Extra crazy! ☐ Survival Mode ☐ OK

☐ Good ☐ Super easy!

Baby's Mood	Your Mood
☹ 😐 😐 🙂 😊	☹ 😐 😐 🙂 😊

Date

....

Notes for Today

_____
_____
_____
_____
_____
_____
_____
_____
_____

Feeding

_____
_____
_____

Changing

_____
_____
_____

Sleep/Naps

_____
_____
_____

Parent's Day: ☐ Extra crazy! ☐ Survival Mode ☐ OK

☐ Good ☐ Super easy!

Baby's Mood	Your Mood
☹ 😐 😐 🙂 😊	☹ 😐 😐 🙂 😊

Date

....

Notes for Today

_____
_____
_____
_____
_____
_____
_____
_____
_____

Feeding

_____
_____

Changing

_____
_____

Sleep/Naps

_____
_____

Parent's Day: ☐ Extra crazy! ☐ Survival Mode ☐ OK
☐ Good ☐ Super easy!

Baby's Mood	Your Mood
☹ ☹ ☺ ☺ ☺	☹ ☹ ☺ ☺ ☺

Date

....

Notes for Today

_____
_____
_____
_____
_____
_____
_____
_____
_____
_____

Feeding

_____
_____

Changing

_____
_____

Sleep/Naps

_____
_____

Parent's Day: ☐ Extra crazy! ☐ Survival Mode ☐ OK

☐ Good ☐ Super easy!

Baby's Mood	Your Mood
☹ 😕 😐 🙂 😊	☹ 😕 😐 🙂 😊

Date

....

Notes for Today

_____
_____
_____
_____
_____
_____
_____
_____

Feeding

_____
_____

Changing

_____
_____

Sleep/Naps

_____
_____

Parent's Day: ☐ Extra crazy! ☐ Survival Mode ☐ OK

☐ Good ☐ Super easy!

Baby's Mood	Your Mood
☹ 😕 😐 🙂 😊	☹ 😕 😐 🙂 😊

Date

....

Notes for Today

_____
_____
_____
_____
_____
_____
_____
_____

Feeding

_____
_____

Changing

_____
_____

Sleep/Naps

_____
_____

Parent's Day: ☐ Extra crazy! ☐ Survival Mode ☐ OK
☐ Good ☐ Super easy!

Baby's Mood	Your Mood
☹ 😕 😐 🙂 ☺	☹ 😕 😐 🙂 ☺

Date

....

Notes for Today

_____
_____
_____
_____
_____
_____
_____
_____
_____
_____

Feeding

_____
_____

Changing

_____
_____

Sleep/Naps

_____
_____

Parent's Day: ☐ Extra crazy! ☐ Survival Mode ☐ OK

☐ Good ☐ Super easy!

Baby's Mood	Your Mood
☹ 😕 😐 🙂 😊	☹ 😕 😐 🙂 😊

Date

....

Notes for Today

_____
_____
_____
_____
_____
_____
_____
_____
_____
_____

Feeding

_____
_____

Changing

_____
_____

Sleep/Naps

_____
_____

Parent's Day: ☐ Extra crazy! ☐ Survival Mode ☐ OK

☐ Good ☐ Super easy!

Baby's Mood	Your Mood
☹ ☹ ☺ ☺ ☺	☹ ☹ ☺ ☺ ☺

Date

....

Notes for Today

_____
_____
_____
_____
_____
_____
_____
_____
_____

Feeding

_____
_____
_____

Changing

_____
_____
_____

Sleep/Naps

_____
_____
_____

Parent's Day: ☐ Extra crazy! ☐ Survival Mode ☐ OK

☐ Good ☐ Super easy!

Baby's Mood	Your Mood

Date

....

Notes for Today

_____
_____
_____
_____
_____
_____
_____
_____
_____

Feeding

_____
_____
_____

Changing

_____
_____
_____

Sleep/Naps

_____
_____
_____

Parent's Day: ☐ Extra crazy! ☐ Survival Mode ☐ OK
☐ Good ☐ Super easy!

Baby's Mood	Your Mood
☹ 😕 😐 🙂 😊	☹ 😕 😐 🙂 😊

Date

···

Notes for Today

_____
_____
_____
_____
_____
_____
_____
_____
_____

Feeding

_____
_____

Changing

_____
_____

Sleep/Naps

_____
_____

Parent's Day: ☐ Extra crazy! ☐ Survival Mode ☐ OK
☐ Good ☐ Super easy!

Baby's Mood	Your Mood
☹ ☺ ☺ ☺ ☺	☹ ☺ ☺ ☺ ☺

Date

....

Notes for Today

_____
_____
_____
_____
_____
_____
_____
_____
_____
_____

Feeding

_____
_____
_____

Changing

_____
_____
_____

Sleep/Naps

_____
_____
_____

Parent's Day: ☐ Extra crazy! ☐ Survival Mode ☐ OK

☐ Good ☐ Super easy!

Baby's Mood	Your Mood
☹ 😐 😐 🙂 😊	☹ 😐 😐 🙂 😊

Date

....

Notes for Today

_____
_____
_____
_____
_____
_____
_____
_____
_____
_____

Feeding

_____
_____
_____

Changing

_____
_____
_____

Sleep/Naps

_____
_____
_____

Parent's Day: ☐ Extra crazy! ☐ Survival Mode ☐ OK

☐ Good ☐ Super easy!

Baby's Mood	Your Mood
☹ 😐 😐 🙂 😊	☹ 😐 😐 🙂 😊

Date

....

Notes for Today

_____
_____
_____
_____
_____
_____
_____
_____
_____
_____

Feeding

_____
_____
_____

Changing

_____
_____
_____

Sleep/Naps

_____
_____
_____

Parent's Day: ☐ Extra crazy! ☐ Survival Mode ☐ OK
☐ Good ☐ Super easy!

Baby's Mood
☹ 😕 😐 🙂 😊

Your Mood
☹ 😕 😐 🙂 😊

Date

....

Notes for Today

_____
_____
_____
_____
_____
_____
_____
_____
_____

Feeding

_____
_____

Changing

_____
_____

Sleep/Naps

_____
_____

Parent's Day: ☐ Extra crazy!   ☐ Survival Mode   ☐ OK

☐ Good   ☐ Super easy!

Baby's Mood   Your Mood

☹ 😕 😐 🙂 😊   ☹ 😕 😐 🙂 😊

Date

....

Notes for Today

_____
_____
_____
_____
_____
_____
_____
_____
_____
_____

Feeding

_____
_____
_____

Changing

_____
_____
_____

Sleep/Naps

_____
_____
_____

Parent's Day: ☐ Extra crazy! ☐ Survival Mode ☐ OK
☐ Good ☐ Super easy!

Baby's Mood   Your Mood
☹ 😕 😐 🙂 😊   ☹ 😕 😐 🙂 😊

Date

··

Notes for Today

_____
_____
_____
_____
_____
_____
_____
_____
_____

Feeding

_____
_____

Changing

_____
_____

Sleep/Naps

_____
_____

Parent's Day: ☐ Extra crazy! ☐ Survival Mode ☐ OK

☐ Good ☐ Super easy!

Baby's Mood	Your Mood
😣 😖 😐 🙂 😊	😣 😖 😐 🙂 😊

Date

·····································

Notes for Today

_____
_____
_____
_____
_____
_____
_____
_____
_____
_____

Feeding

_____
_____
_____

Changing

_____
_____
_____

Sleep/Naps

_____
_____
_____

Parent's Day: ☐ Extra crazy! ☐ Survival Mode ☐ OK

☐ Good ☐ Super easy!

Baby's Mood	Your Mood
☹ 😕 😐 🙂 😊	☹ 😕 😐 🙂 😊

Date

....

Notes for Today

_____
_____
_____
_____
_____
_____
_____
_____
_____

Feeding

_____
_____

Changing

_____
_____

Sleep/Naps

_____
_____

Parent's Day: ☐ Extra crazy! ☐ Survival Mode ☐ OK
☐ Good ☐ Super easy!

Baby's Mood	Your Mood
☹ ☹ ☺ ☺ ☺	☹ ☹ ☺ ☺ ☺

Date

....

Notes for Today

_____
_____
_____
_____
_____
_____
_____
_____
_____

Feeding

_____
_____

Changing

_____
_____

Sleep/Naps

_____
_____

Parent's Day: ☐ Extra crazy! ☐ Survival Mode ☐ OK

☐ Good ☐ Super easy!

Baby's Mood

☹ 😐 😐 🙂 😊

Your Mood

☹ 😐 😐 🙂 😊

Date

....

Notes for Today

_____
_____
_____
_____
_____
_____
_____
_____
_____
_____

Feeding

_____
_____
_____

Changing

_____
_____
_____

Sleep/Naps

_____
_____
_____

Parent's Day: ☐ Extra crazy! ☐ Survival Mode ☐ OK
              ☐ Good   ☐ Super easy!

Baby's Mood	Your Mood
☹ ☺ ☺ ☺ ☺	☹ ☺ ☺ ☺ ☺

Date

....

Notes for Today

_____
_____
_____
_____
_____
_____
_____
_____
_____
_____

Feeding

_____
_____
_____

Changing

_____
_____
_____

Sleep/Naps

_____
_____
_____

Parent's Day: ☐ Extra crazy! ☐ Survival Mode ☐ OK

☐ Good ☐ Super easy!

Baby's Mood	Your Mood
☹ 😐 😐 🙂 😊	☹ 😐 😐 🙂 😊

Date

....

Notes for Today

_____
_____
_____
_____
_____
_____
_____
_____
_____
_____

Feeding

_____
_____

Changing

_____
_____

Sleep/Naps

_____
_____

Parent's Day: ☐ Extra crazy! ☐ Survival Mode ☐ OK

☐ Good ☐ Super easy!

Baby's Mood	Your Mood

Date

....

Notes for Today

_____
_____
_____
_____
_____
_____
_____
_____
_____

Feeding

_____
_____

Changing

_____
_____

Sleep/Naps

_____
_____

Parent's Day: ☐ Extra crazy! ☐ Survival Mode ☐ OK
☐ Good ☐ Super easy!

Baby's Mood ☹ ☺ ☺ ☺ ☺ : Your Mood ☹ ☺ ☺ ☺ ☺

Date

....

Notes for Today

_____
_____
_____
_____
_____
_____
_____
_____
_____

Feeding

_____
_____

Changing

_____
_____

Sleep/Naps

_____
_____

Parent's Day: ☐ Extra crazy! ☐ Survival Mode ☐ OK

☐ Good ☐ Super easy!

Baby's Mood	Your Mood
☹ 😐 😐 😐 ☺	☹ 😐 😐 😐 ☺

Date

....

Notes for Today

_____
_____
_____
_____
_____
_____
_____
_____
_____

Feeding
_____
_____

Changing
_____
_____

Sleep/Naps
_____
_____

Parent's Day: ☐ Extra crazy! ☐ Survival Mode ☐ OK
☐ Good ☐ Super easy!

Baby's Mood	Your Mood
☹ ☺ ☺ ☺ ☺	☹ ☺ ☺ ☺ ☺

Date

....

Notes for Today

_____
_____
_____
_____
_____
_____
_____
_____
_____
_____

Feeding
_____
_____

Changing
_____
_____

Sleep/Naps
_____
_____

Parent's Day: ☐ Extra crazy! ☐ Survival Mode ☐ OK
☐ Good ☐ Super easy!

Baby's Mood	Your Mood
😣 😖 😐 🙂 😊	😣 😖 😐 🙂 😊

Monthly Progress

Babies are always more trouble than you thought
—and more wonderful.

CHARLES OSGOOD

BABY'S PROGRESS * *Month 1* ....

Weight _____

Height _____

Highlights

_____
_____
_____
_____
_____
_____
_____
_____

Month 2 ....

Weight _____

Height _____

Highlights

_____
_____
_____
_____
_____
_____
_____
_____

Month 3 ....

Weight _____   Height _____

Highlights

_____
_____
_____
_____
_____
_____
_____
_____

Month 4 ....

Weight _____   Height _____

Highlights

_____
_____
_____
_____
_____
_____
_____
_____

BABY'S PROGRESS * *Month 5* ....

Weight _____   Height _____

Highlights

_____
_____
_____
_____
_____
_____
_____
_____

Month 6 ....

Weight _____   Height _____

Highlights

_____
_____
_____
_____
_____
_____
_____
_____

Month 7 ....

Weight _____

Height _____

Highlights

_____
_____
_____
_____
_____
_____
_____
_____

Month 8 ....

Weight _____

Height _____

Highlights

_____
_____
_____
_____
_____
_____
_____
_____

BABY'S PROGRESS * *Month 9* ....

Weight _____

Height _____

Highlights

_____
_____
_____
_____
_____
_____
_____

Month 10 ....

Weight _____

Height _____

Highlights

_____
_____
_____
_____
_____
_____
_____

Month 11 ....

Weight _____

Height _____

Highlights

_____
_____
_____
_____
_____
_____
_____
_____

Month 12 ....

Weight _____

Height _____

Highlights

_____
_____
_____
_____
_____
_____
_____
_____

BABY'S PROGRESS * Month 13 ....

Weight _____

Height _____

Highlights

_____
_____
_____
_____
_____
_____
_____

PLACE BABY'S
FIRST BIRTHDAY PHOTO HERE!

Notes

Notes

Notes

Notes

Notes

Notes